The CHORAL CONDUCTOR'S HANDBOOK

by
WALTER EHRET

EDWARD B. MARKS MUSIC COMPANY

EXCLUSIVELY DISTRIBUTED BY
HAL•LEONARD®

To my Teacher and Friend
HARRY ROBERT WILSON

CONTENTS

FOREWORD

This digest of the fundamentals of the choral art is designed to be of help to all choral directors regardless of their experience and ability, or the skill of their groups.

The chapters are set up to cover one problem area at a time. The suggested solutions in each area are stated succinctly. Should the reader wish extended information on any point, he should refer to any standard text. Of course, the suggested devices must be used with good judgment since the musical content and form, as well as the performing group, will govern their application. Many of the points are made as definite statements for purposes of clarity and should be applied with this in mind.

The book is a collection of ideas, procedures and devices which have been successfully used with choral groups of all ages. The veteran conductor may use it as a check list for his own work — the less experienced conductor will find the material of great value both in building a fine chorus as well as in developing an increased awareness and sensitivity on his own part.

The handbook may well serve as a text for choral conducting classes as well as a source book of information for members of school, community and church groups.

WALTER EHRET

CHAPTER **1**

REHEARSAL PROCEDURES

ORGANIZATIONAL DETAILS.

1 START ON TIME.

2 THE BEST TIME TO SCHEDULE YOUR REHEARSAL is in the late morning.

3 TWO 40-45 MINUTE PERIODS are more fruitful than one period lasting the same total amount of time.

4 SELECTIONS TO BE REHEARSED SHOULD BE LISTED ON THE BOARD IN ORDER OF REHEARSAL. Choristers should set up their music as soon as they are seated.

5 MAKE OUT A WORK PLAN with a definite time schedule and adhere to it.

6 HAVE COMPETENT STUDENT ASSISTANTS set up the rehearsal room, pass out music, check attendance, do library work, etc.

7 HAVE YOUR FILES AND LIBRARY ACCESSIBLE to the rehearsal room.

8 GIVE THE SELECTION TO YOUR ACCOMPANIST BEFORE THE FIRST REHEARSAL for prior study. Go over it with the accompanist *before* the rehearsal. At this time tempi should be established and mistakes corrected. Group time should not be wasted in two-way discussions between director and accompanist.

Ask private piano teachers to cooperate by using these accompaniments as part of the piano lesson assignment. Parents can also be helpful.

9 THE PIANO SHOULD BE SO PLACED THAT THE ACCOMPANIST CAN SEE YOU CLEARLY.

10 THE LIBRARIAN SHOULD MARK ALL OF THE CHORISTERS' COPIES, highlighting special directions, such as staggered breathing, special changes of voicings, (the altos singing with tenors on a certain passage), rehearsal numbers, etc.

Each member should have his *own* set of music so that additional *personal* markings can be made.

11 ARRANGE TO HAVE AT LEAST ONE MALE AND ONE FEMALE SECTIONAL REHEARSAL for every two or three mixed rehearsals.

12 DEVELOP STUDENT LEADERS. They can assist by leading sectionals, drilling and rehearsing small ensembles, preparing soloists, coaching weak members, etc.

13 IF REHEARSAL TIME IS LIMITED, ORGANIZE EXTRA "READING REHEARSALS" or form a "Choral Reading Club." Graded sight reading courses are most helpful and a little time spent on such activities increases efficiency in learning new music.*

Have a "sight reading sing", involving local community and church groups as well as your own chorus. Each director should be responsible for providing a certain number of copies of a few of his "favorite" choral works. Each of the directors leads the combined groups in the selections he has brought. For variety, each group could sing one "solo" number, thus providing a "breather" for the others.

For a finale, the groups could sing one special selection that has been chosen in advance and *prepared* by all those participating. A rousing finale such as this could provide a thrilling conclusion of the evening.

If budgets are limited, community song books provide material for reading and are inexpensive additions to a choral library. In addition to the items usually

*SEE AND SING — Ehret, Vol. I, II, III. Pro Art Publ.

found in such collections, many newly released community song books include outstanding concert choral works in original versions. While written in close score, they can nevertheless be used as program material.

14 A "BREAK" DURING THE REHEARSAL IS ADVISABLE, particularly after a period of intense concentration. In a typical 45 minute rehearsal, allow for a 1-2 minute "stretch" and "gab" period. In a longer rehearsal (2 hours, etc.) allow for a complete five to ten minute break.

   a) Some directors give their groups a "break" by a complete change in the type of music being sung and allow them to do a bit of "barber shopping" or a little free harmonization on a popular tune.

   b) Have a member of the chorus sing a prepared solo during these "breaks". These solo spots should be given to those not possessing solo voices and who might never sing before a large audience.

   c) Try "sight reading" a short, easy choral work during a "break".

   d) Borrow reading material from other school, church, and community groups.

15 SERVE LIGHT REFRESHMENTS AT ONE OF YOUR "EXTRA" EVENING REHEARSALS and make that rehearsal more fun to attend.

16 STAND UP OCCASIONALLY.

FOR THE DIRECTOR

1 CENTER YOUR ATTENTION ON THE GROUP and not on the score. This means that the conductor *must* have learned the music *before* the *first* rehearsal.

2 DO NOT START THE GROUP WITH A "ONE, TWO, THREE, SING." Use a simple upbeat as you would if directing professionals. Amateur singers can be conditioned to responding to a preparatory beat and a down beat. Use practice attacks at different speeds and dynamic levels to make choristers aware of the conductor.

3 INJECT HUMOR INTO YOUR REHEARSAL. This is particularly important when tensions mount, as in the "home stretch" before an important appearance. Have on tap a fund of humorous stories relative to the choral art.

4 ENCOURAGE! An overly critical, negative approach can lower the morale of the group and do immeasurable harm. This is not a plea for lower standards, but a suggestion that the director be fully aware of the effects of consistent and strong criticism.

5 SING FOR, BUT NOT WITH THE GROUP.

6 DO NOT ALLOW MINOR INFRACTIONS TO PASS or they will mushroom into larger ones and become established habits.

7 TALKING SHOULD CEASE INSTANTLY AS THE CONDUCTOR STEPS BEFORE THE GROUP. Instructions should be given only when there is absolute quiet. An orderly, well run rehearsal is a strong factor in contributing to the morale of a group. Non-cooperative individuals should be dismissed. No one person is more important than the group.

8 STUDY AND MARK YOUR SCORE thoroughly *before* the first rehearsal.

9 TALK LITTLE, SING MUCH!

10 DO NOT ACTUALLY CONDUCT UNTIL A FAIR CONTROL OF THE WORK IS ATTAINED. Never over-conduct at any rehearsal. Always leave something in reserve for the performance.

11 TEACH PRINCIPLES AND NOT CASES.

12 DEMONSTRATION IS AN EFFICIENT WAY TO MAKE A POINT.

GROUP RESPONSE

1 CHORISTERS SHOULD NOT BE AFRAID OF MAKING MISTAKES. They should, on the contrary, be encouraged to make "good" ones. A well-defined mistake can be corrected more easily than one which is made timidly and therefore never quite establishes itself as right or wrong.

2 CHORUS MEMBERS SHOULD REQUEST REHEARSAL OF SPECIFIC SECTIONS OF A COMPOSITION. A section that bothers one person usually has difficulties for others.

3 WHEN THE GROUP BECOMES TIRED OR RESTLESS, VARY YOUR PROCEDURES OR MATERIALS.

4 CHORISTERS SHOULD THINK FOR THEMSELVES. Invite them to make suggestions relative to climaxes, mood, color, dynamics, tempi, etc. In the beginning this procedure appears to be time consuming, but eventually, increased awareness and sensitivity will develop. The result is a higher level of group musicianship. It is advisable to incorporate such group suggestions into the interpretation if they make good sense. A chorister whose suggestion is used will identify himself with the work to an extent that could not be brought about by any other means.

5 CHORUS MEMBERS MUST WATCH OTHER PARTS OF THE SCORE WHILE SINGING. Most singers are *one part* conscious and never *see* or *hear* themselves in relation to the entire tonal structure.

Each singer should know every other part almost as well as his own. It is good practice to deliberately switch parts and have the sections sing parts other than their own. For example, tenors sing the soprano part, altos sing the tenor part, etc. Although aesthetically unsatisfactory, this device will liven up the rehearsal and, at the same time, serve to increase reading skill. This could be a D.D.D. (Dull Day Device.)

6 CHORISTERS MUST BE MADE AWARE OF THE NEED FOR A 100% START ON ATTACKS. Laggards and stragglers should be dealt with severely for their inertia since they are responsible for the "false start", one of the most pernicious time wasters of the choral rehearsal.

7 CENSURE THOSE WHO CONTINUE SINGING AFTER A STOP HAS BEEN INDICATED. This is gross inattention and is never to be condoned.

8 SINGERS SHOULD SIT IN EITHER OF TWO GENERALLY ACCEPTED POSITIONS:
   a) On the front two inches of the seat, torso erect, spine straight, no protuberance of the abdominal area, both feet firmly "gripping" the floor with one foot slightly in advance of the other so that the entire body is in a position of balance. This position is preferable.
   b) Body firmly fixed completely against the back of the chair with as erect a position of the torso as is possible.
   Directors may alternate these two positions during the course of a rehearsal.

9 CHORISTERS SHOULD HOLD THE MUSIC UP, WITH THE ARMS AWAY FROM THE BODY. If the music is down in the lap, it is difficult for the singer to direct visual attention to the conductor. Also, this position is not conducive to proper breathing, which is fundamental to good vocal production. Finally, because of poor body balance, conditions of tension in neck and throat arise and contribute to faulty quality, poor pitch, limited range, and to poor singing in general.

10 ALL CHORUS MEMBERS SHOULD BE FAMILIAR WITH AND ABLE TO CONDUCT THE STANDARD BEATS
$$\frac{2}{4}, \frac{3}{4}, \frac{4}{4} \text{ and } \frac{6}{8}.$$

If a member of the group shows any conducting ability, turn over part or all of a rehearsal to him. A good student director will get assiduous attention from the group and will provide the director with an opportunity to work within the group while the rehearsal is going on. This student should be allowed to conduct a number or two at a public performance.

11 SINGERS SHOULD WATCH NOTES AND SYMBOLS (*f, p,* etc.) NOT WORDS. The text will usually be seen peripherally.

REHEARSAL TECHNIQUES
and
GROUP DEVELOPMENT

1 DO NOT REPEAT A PHRASE FOR "NOTES" ONLY. All repetitions should involve working on the implications of text, dynamics, and tonal features, as well as musical style.

2 ACCOMPANISTS SHOULD PLAY THE STARTING CHORD SOFTLY. Singers can be trained to pick their parts out of a chord. Insist that the singers *hum* the starting chord to indicate that all is set.

3 AFTER A SELECTION HAS BEEN FAIRLY WELL LEARNED, TRANSPOSE IT TO DIFFERENT KEYS FOR A CAPPELLA VOCALIZATION. Most compositions can be sung as much as a minor third higher or lower without undue strain. The height or depth of an individual part will determine the limit of transposition.

Accompanied as well as unaccompanied numbers should be practiced *without* piano. Weaknesses, rhythmic and otherwise, will thus be quickly revealed. Unaccompanied practice puts a premium on more attentive listening and develops greater accuracy, assurance, and self reliance.

4 TO SUGGEST A DIFFICULTY IS TO CREATE ONE. Many "problems" are usually in the conductor's mind. The average amateur choristers can usually learn any work the conductor is able to teach them.

5 GIVE SPECIAL ATTENTION TO THE MALE VOICES. Fuzz and muddiness in the tonal mass is usually the result of inaccuracy in the lower parts.

6 ELABORATE DIRECTIONS GIVEN BEFORE STARTING WILL INVARIABLY BE FORGOTTEN. One or two succinct points are in order, however.

7 EACH REHEARSAL SHOULD CONCLUDE WITH A FEELING OF ACCOMPLISHMENT. Use the last few minutes of every rehearsal to present a brief recapitulation of points covered, those mastered, and those yet to be improved.

8 DO NOT DEVELOP A FIXED PATTERN OF REHEARSAL PROCEDURES. Vary the procedure from day to day.

9 IF A PASSAGE IS DIFFICULT AND IS NOT CLARIFIED BY REPETITION, TRY SEPARATING THE PROBLEM INTO ITS COMPONENT PARTS. For example, if a passage contains unusual melodic intervals in combination with unusual rhythms, you should:

    a) Sing the intervals *without reference to rhythm,* using long tones until each note is secure.

    b) Chant or speak the text in the written rhythm.

    c) Combine notes and text in the rhythm indicated in the score.

10 TRY THE FOLLOWING WAYS TO START A REHEARSAL:

    a) Have the accompanist start playing as the rehearsal begins. As the choristers enter, they should start humming their parts, continuing until the entire group has entered the room.

b) Use a choral recording to start the rehearsal. The playing starts as the period begins and the choristers take their places quietly so that they may be able to listen. This recording may be a professional one by an outstanding group or it may be a tape of a previous rehearsal by the group itself.

11 DO NOT SPEND TOO MUCH TIME ON ONE SECTION OR PIECE AT A REHEARSAL. There is always a point of diminishing returns and the wise director knows when that point is reached. Move on to something else and you will find that the problems may have resolved themselves by the time of the next rehearsal.

12 VARY ALL DRILLS AND REPETITIONS by having Solo, Duet, Trio, or Quartet combinations perform instead of the section or sections. Each rehearsal should provide the opportunity for an individual, or group of individuals to perform.

Provide friendly competition within the group as follows:

a) Seniors against the Juniors.

b) Freshmen and Seniors against Sophomores and Juniors.

c) Girls who didn't wash the supper dishes against those who did, etc.

13 DO NOT REHEARSE ONE SECTION WHILE OTHERS REMAIN IDLE. Have the other sections participate in some way. If, for example, the tenors are having trouble, ask all members to sing the tenor part or softly hum their own parts.

14 IT IS ACCEPTABLE TO VOCALIZE A GROUP FOR A FEW MINUTES AT THE BEGINNING OF A REHEARSAL, but it should be kept in mind that most vocalization, in order to be functional, should be drawn from the music being studied. The choir members must always see the purpose for any specific vocalization and must understand its relationship to the work being studied.

Isolated vocalizing for purely basic vocal reasons is not out of order, but is less significant than the singing of exercises having direct connection with the learning of the repertoire.

15 USE "ERRATIC CONDUCTING" when your group becomes sluggish. Deliberate distortion of tempi, ridiculous stops, meaningless holds, accordion-like dynamics, etc., make for fun and profit by increased awareness of the conductor and additional sensitivity to him. (Dull Day Device.)

16 REHEARSE SELECTIONS THAT ARE WRITTEN EITHER FOR MALE OR FEMALE VOICES. This varies an unusually long rehearsal and provides an opportunity to rest voices. Too many choral programs include mixed voice selections only. Plan to have a group of male and female settings on each program.

17 DO NOT TRY TO LEARN A NUMBER IN ONE OR TWO SUCCESSIVE REHEARSALS. Work simultaneously on several numbers in various stages of development. This not only provides variety, but also differing levels of work intensity and concentration.

18 REHEARSE A SELECTION IN DIFFERENT PLACES ON SUCCESSIVE REHEARSAL DAYS. Do not always start at the beginning and work from that point. At each rehearsal take advantage of the group's initial freshness by rehearsing a section not covered previously. It is helpful to mark copies with rehearsal numbers.

19 WHEN MAKING CORRECTIONS IN ANY GIVEN PART, MAKE THEM IN SUCH A WAY THAT ALL CAN HEAR THEM. All members should feel that the correction applies to them as well as to the section being corrected.

20 DO NOT MAKE CHORISTERS SING IN THE UPPER QUARTER OF THEIR RANGES FOR A LONG PERIOD OF TIME.

21 SINGERS SHOULD NOT PRACTICE FORTISSIMO PASSAGES EXCESSIVELY. Rehearse such passages at a mezzo forte level until learned.

22 DO NOT SPEND TOO MUCH TIME REHEARSING THE MOST PLEASING AND LEAST DIFFICULT PORTIONS OF ANY WORK. Face the problems, isolate them, and solve them.

23 CORRECT MISTAKES AS SOON AS POSSIBLE. While this seems to be an obviously elementary precept, many directors allow a passage to be sung repeatedly, hoping that, through mere repetition, notes or passages will correct themselves. While self correction takes place in many advanced groups, this is the exception rather than the rule. Remember, something learned incorrectly is difficult to "unlearn".

24 WHEN CORRECTING WRONG NOTES, point out the difference between what has been sung incorrectly and what is correct.

25 MEMORIZE WHILE LEARNING, *not after* the selection is "learned". An efficient, mentally alert rehearsal brings about memorization from the *very beginning*. Too often the music is allowed to remain in the hands of the chorus members for *far too long a period of time*.

From the moment of the first repetition that initiates the learning process, the score should be used only for *occasional* reference. Practically all rehearsing can be done with the eyes away from the music and on the director — *if the director so insists*.

Aids in memorization:
  a) After the third repeat of any phrase or section, insist that it be performed from *memory* thereafter.
  b) Set up short range goals, such as "at the end of four rehearsals you will perform these two numbers from memory without a stop". This short term motivation acts as a very strong incentive to most groups and intensifies the learning process.

26 IF THE PIANO MUST BE USED AT REHEARSAL:
  a) Play softly.
  b) Do not play percussively.
  c) In accompanying, do not play constantly. Strike only an occasional chord, preferably the strong beats of a measure, mark harmonic changes, etc.
  d) When the female parts are being sung alone, play the male parts, and vice versa.
  e) Occasionally play notes in a different octave from that being sung. For example, if the group is singing a staccato passage, a lighter feeling is created if, during practice, the piano accompaniment is played one octave higher.

27 CHORISTERS SHOULD BE SENSITIVE TO SMALL CONDUCTING MOVEMENTS RATHER THAN TO LARGE ONES. Maximum response to minimum movement should be the goal. Save larger motion for climactic sections that call for voluminous or dramatic effects.

28 ALWAYS GIVE A REASON FOR ANY REPETITION. Out with "Let's do it again".

29 AVOID VAGUE GENERALIZATIONS, such as "Tenors were flat". Tell the Tenors *exactly* where and why they were out of tune and correct them.

30 REHEARSALS SHOULD NOT BE CONFINED TO WORKS THAT ARE GOING TO BE PERFORMED. Devote some rehearsal time to the *sight reading* of easy but worthwhile choral literature.

31 ADDITIONAL REHEARSALS SHOULD BE REQUIRED FOR THE WEAKER MEMBERS OF THE GROUP. These can be assigned individually or in small groups. Such help periods can be directed by the accompanist or a student conductor, with an occasional check by the director. Rehearsals should be held regularly and not just before performances.

32 BE EXPLICIT IN DIRECTIONS. It is wise to start with the larger area and become more definitive:

a) Page

b) Line

c) Measure

d) Beat (or word)

If the work has rehearsal numbers or letters, these, of course, should be used. If they are not printed, have your librarian add them in red pencil.

33 DO NOT ALWAYS GO BACK TO A GIVEN REHEARSAL NUMBER OR LETTER when you wish to rehearse a few measures somewhere *between* two specific rehearsal numbers. Far too much rehearsal time is consumed in singing measures that *do not need rehearsing* in order to lead into the measures that require attention. An *alert* group *can* and *must* be conditioned to start at any given measure and proceed from that point.

It should be pointed out, however, that once these few measures are under control, it is advisable to go back to the preceeding rehearsal number and sing from that point past the area of difficulty to ascertain whether or not complete harmonic and rhythmic continuity has been established.

34 MAKE CERTAIN YOUR GROUP IS AT ATTENTION BEFORE GIVING DIRECTIONS. Do not repeat directions for the inattentive.

35 IN ADDITION TO PERFORMING PART ARRANGEMENTS, DO NOT NEGLECT THE UNISON SONG, a valuable ensemble trainer. A good unison is the first requisite of good ensemble. In addition to one pitch, it implies one quality, one vowel sound, one color, one dynamic level, etc. Occasionally include a unison selection on your program.

36 IF ANY SECTION IS HAVING DIFFICULTY HOLDING ITS PART, MAKE THAT PART "STAND OUT" by using some of the following devices:

a) Have the weak section sing with *words* while the others *hum* or use neutral syllables.

b) All parts, except the one having difficulty, sing softly.

c) Practice the part having difficulty, using piano accompaniment only.

d) If there is general insecurity in *all* parts, have *each section* sing with a different neutral vowel sound. Thus:

Sopranos on NAH.

Altos on NEE.

Tenors on NOH.

Basses on NOO, etc.

In this way the definitive quality of these "sectional" vowels will hold the sections together within themselves while the completeness of the four part harmony will still be retained.

37 IF A NUMBER JUST DOES NOT GO AFTER A REASONABLE REHEARSAL PERIOD, DROP IT!

38 EACH CHOIR SHOULD HAVE CONTROL OF AT LEAST FOUR VARYING STYLES OF DELIVERY OR ARTICULATION:

a) *Legato* — Notes smoothly connected without separation of any kind. No slurring or sliding between notes; however, try to remove all feeling of bar line or accent.

b) *Semi-Legato* — Think legato, but aspirate each note slightly, giving a slight lift and separation to each note.

c) *Semi-Staccato* — Think staccato, but do not leave as much space between notes as you would in staccato singing.

d) *Staccato* — Sharply detached, with as much *space* as possible between each note. *Marcato*, an outgrowth of staccato (or vice versa), is usually more heavily executed with emphasis on the *notes* rather than on the *space* between the notes.

All other articulations are extensions or modifications of these four styles.

To develop a "feel" for these contrasting articulations, use scale or chord exercises in the following way:

1. Sing *legato* — Think Smoothly; no sliding between notes.

Ah _____ Ah _____

2. Sing *semi-legato* — Think *legato*, but insert an "H" before every note.

Hah hah hah hah hah hah hah hah   Hah hah hah hah hah hah hah hah

3. Sing *staccato* — It is best to establish this *before* going back to *semi-staccato*. All notes must be *cleanly separated*. Think space between the notes. Sing lightly.

Hah hah hah hah hah hah hah hah   Hah hah hah hah hah hah hah hah

4. Sing *semi-staccato* — Think *staccato*, but lengthen *slightly* the individual notes.

Hah hah hah hah hah hah hah hah   Hah hah hah hah hah hah hah hah

The chief problem of articulation will be to differentiate between *semi-legato* and *semi-staccato*, but practice should clarify this subtle difference in a short period of time.

5. It should be pointed out that in individual voice parts of a piece of music the articulations are not always identical. For example, the sopranos may have a legato passage while the accompanying voices have a *semi-staccato* articulation. Search carefully for moments of articulatory contrast. Some interesting vocal effects can be derived from such stylistic differences.

39 SING ONE SELECTION STANDING UP AT EACH REHEARSAL.

40 ALTERNATE DIFFICULT AND EASY NUMBERS during one rehearsal period. You should have many varied selections in work at the same time (style, difficulty, key, mood, range, etc.).

41 WHEN PRACTICING IN AN AUDITORIUM, STEP AWAY FROM THE GROUP and listen to it from a distance. Many things will be discovered which would otherwise be overlooked. Allow members of the group to hear the chorus from afar. Weaknesses not apparent to them when they are within the group will be   evidence when they hear it from a distance.

42 CHOIRS AS A UNIT BREATHE TOO MUCH! There is no valid reason for a unison breath in the middle of a long phrase or before a climax note. Instruct your members in the use of "staggered" or "relay" breathing and enjoy the pleasure of a "long" phrase, the control of which is basic to superior choral singing.

The rules for staggered breathing are simple and easily mastered.

STAGGERED BREATHING — GENERAL PRINCIPLES:
   a) Breathe *more* frequently than you would in a phrase of regular length. In the beginning the chorister will sing as long as he can on one breath until exhausted, then take a fast breath (usually shallow) and sing until all air is expelled. This results in tensions and fatigues the singer. In staggered breathing, breaths are taken fully, easily, and often.
   b) As you leave a vowel in the middle of a word, make certain that you return on that same vowel. Merely leave the mouth in the same position and inhale.
   c) After a breath, make certain that you re-enter at the same dynamic level. The tendency is to return to the note with a little more volume. These uncontrolled dynamic bulges can be most annoying, particularly when the choir is singing softly. In the beginning it is advisable to return at a *lower* dynamic level and subtly bring the voice up to the group level.

STAGGERED BREATHING — SPECIFIC RULES:
Where *not* to breathe:
   a) Over a bar.
   b) After a long note and directly before a group of short notes.
   c) At the end of a phrase.
   d) At a "danger" spot. Danger spots are specially indicated areas about which the group has been cautioned by the director.
   e) Before a jump to a high note.
Where to breathe:
   a) In the middle of a long note, coming back again to that note after the catch breath is *taken*.
   b) In the middle of a word.
   c) Directly after the person next to you has taken a breath.
   d) When singing melismatic passages that move rapidly, the singer will *omit* one or several of the notes as he breathes.

HOW TO ORGANIZE A CHOIR "STAGGERED BREATHING" SET-UP:
   Divide the group into four divisions (alphabetically, according to the last name). Assign these four divisions as follows:
   a) First quarter (alphabetically) breathes any place in the *first third* of any *measure*.
   b) Second quarter (alphabetically) breathes any place in the *second third* of any *measure*.

c) Third quarter (alphabetically) breathes any place in the *last third* of any *measure*.

d) Fourth quarter (alphabetically) breathes any place following the rules mentioned previously. This is a "floating" group designed to fill in any holes that may develop.

43 IN SINGING A PHRASE OF NORMAL LENGTH, DO NOT BREATHE IN THE MIDDLE OF A WORD.

44 DO SOME STACCATO VOCALIZATION EACH DAY. This valuable technique is usually neglected as a phase of vocal development. Staccato singing activates the muscles of the diaphragm and is invaluable in relieving the voice of heaviness, languor, and inertia, at the same time adding a degree of buoyancy.

The practicing of choral numbers in staccato manner is invaluable, not only as a device for acquiring the staccato technique, but also to reveal rhythmic weaknesses not always apparent when the selection is sung as written. Pieces of great rhythmic complexity (fugues, and compositions in the polyphonic idiom) are especially adaptable to this type of rendition.

Caution: Staccato singing should not be excessively prolonged as it is tiring and creates throat tensions.

Staccato singing should be executed at a *p* level, or at most *mf*.

CHAPTER **2**

PRESENTING A NEW CHORAL WORK

1 DISCUSS *briefly* the text, composer, style, etc.

2 PLAY the work while the group follows silently. Use recordings if available.

3 PLAY THE WORK AGAIN, allowing the chorus to HUM THE PARTS (or to sing them on a neutral syllable). Encourage them to concentrate on the notes instead of the text.

4 HAVE THE GROUP SING IN PARTS, WITH THE TEXT. Move ahead regardless of breakdowns.

5 ISOLATE AND REHEARSE ANY DIFFICULT INDIVIDUAL PARTS, one at a time, proceeding as follows:
a) Sing bass part (every voice category, including the female voices an octave higher).
b) Sing tenor part (every voice category, including the basses who sing falsetto on high notes).
c) Combine bass and tenor parts (sopranos sing tenor — altos sing bass).
d) Sing alto part (every voice category, including the male voices an octave lower).
e) Combine alto with bass and tenor parts (sopranos sing tenor or alto parts).
f) Sing soprano part (every voice category — basses sing falsetto on high notes).
g) Combine soprano with other parts.

It is possible to shorten this procedure if a particular section has good readers. For example, it may be advisable to do steps *d)* and *f)* simultaneously and then step *g)*. Sometimes two specific parts may be learned together, thus modifying the usual procedure. Example: basses and altos having a unison passage, or tenors and sopranos holding long sustained notes that are rhythmically the same. A study of the score may reveal passages that will require variations of this outlined procedure.

6 REHEARSING ALL PARTS SIMULTANEOUSLY is always most desirable and should be attempted first. In difficult places, whenever serious trouble of any kind develops, the conductor will have to resort to rehearsing individual parts. (See 5).

Points to remember:

a) Learn the melody last. This will serve to eliminate having the tune sung by those who are to sing the harmony.

b) Vary the group combinations when learning selections, i.e., have the sopranos sing their part with the tenors, basses with the altos, tenors with the altos, etc.

c) Each member should sing the other voice parts as well as his own. This singing at all times serves to:

1) keep everyone busy;

2) provide maximum vocal effort;

3) increase awareness of other parts;

4) provide an insight into the difficulties and vocal problems of other parts.

d) While there is usually no problem in having the altos sing the bass part one octave higher, tenors singing bass parts should be told to drop out when ranges become too low. Basses, when singing tenor parts, should be urged either to drop out on high parts or to use a light falsetto for the upper notes. They should not be encouraged to sing the tenor part an octave lower than it sounds.

7 CHANT THE TEXT as a device for learning rhythm, diction, style, dynamics and other related musical and interpretative characteristics.

CHAPTER **3**

FLATTING

PHYSIOLOGICAL
and
PSYCHOLOGICAL CAUSES

1 POOR TONE PRODUCTION usually caused by constriction in and around the base of the tongue, a rigid jaw, and rear production without a feeling of forward resonance and focus. This results in a throaty quality and contributes to flatting in general.

2 LACK OF ADEQUATE BREATH SUPPLY to keep pressure against the vocal chords.

3 POOR POSTURE which interferes with proper breathing.

4 IMPROPER METHOD OF BREATHING. Most competent authorities suggest diaphragmatic breathing.

5 WASTING BREATH by unthinking, uncontrolled attack on the beginning note of a phrase, thus expending too much air initially and not having enough breath left for the remainder of the phrase. This lack of breath support will cause the group to flat. The vocalists' "sights" should be several beats *past* the end of the phrase. A helpful device is to start a few measures from the end of the phrase and gradually add preceding measures until the entire phrase is learned.

6 LACK OF PHYSICAL AND MENTAL ALERTNESS (inertia, both mental and physical). To conquer inertia, find ways to vary and enliven the rehearsal by incorporating new approaches and ideas relative to song study (use of audio aids, etc.).

7 A HEARING PROBLEM. In the case of a member of a school group, a check with the school nurse on the student's past medical history will sometimes reveal causes of vocal problems. If no case history exists and the director *suspects* an aural problem, he should make a referral to the school nurse.

8 OVERLEARNING A SELECTION (going stale). If this is the case, drop the selection for a while and restudy it later with fresh, new approaches. This situation will not occur if the rehearsals are properly planned, spaced, and timed, so that the group is "up" for the performance.

9 "BREAK" OR "LIFT" AREAS IN INDIVIDUAL VOICES are usually intonation trouble spots.

10 WRONG VOICE CLASSIFICATIONS. A heavy baritone singing tenor will, by force of weight as well as the high tessitura, tend to bring down the pitch of the tenor section. This, in turn, will cause the entire group to flat.

11 PHYSICAL AND MENTAL FATIGUE, particularly in evidence before the "big show", following extended vacations, during important examination periods, hot weather, etc. Planning for these times of stress will usually bring the conductor through without much difficulty. A well organized rehearsal program will remove the necessity for strenuous, last minute, extra rehearsals that drain both the performer and director. Efficient rehearsals with specific weekly objectives will bring the group to its peak at the time of performance.

12 CERTAIN NOTES IN EACH VOICE RANGE often demand the attention of the director. While they do not necessarily flat, they can cause trouble.

13 A DEFICIENT EAR will contribute to pitch inaccuracies. By this is meant an ear that needs additional training in hearing and singing whole and half steps particularly.

14 A CHEST TONE QUALITY (low register), carried to the top in awkward, heavy fashion will result not only in harshness of blend, but will tend to pull the group from its intonation moorings. Such cases require individual treatment.

15 CONSTITUTIONAL FLATTERS should be removed from the group, provided, of course, that ample individual help has been given prior to dismissal.

16 TOO MANY HEAVIER TIMBRED VOICES will bring the group pitch down. Fullness, while desirable, must not be obtained at the sacrifice of pitch. The choir should be composed of all varying types of voices; Mezzo, Lyric, Coloratura, Dramatic, etc. These different types will contribute not only to pitch security, but will also provide the conductor with variable tone color resources to draw upon in order to minimize the monochromatic renderings so common to choral performances.

ENVIRONMENTAL CAUSES

1 TOO MUCH HEAT OR POOR VENTILATION. Err in favor of the cooler room.
2 POOR TIME OF DAY FOR REHEARSALS. Early morning is inadvisable because at that time the voices are literally not "warmed up". If possible, rehearsals should be scheduled during late morning, prior to lunch.
3 POOR ACOUSTICS on the stage or in the auditorium which prevent members of the group from hearing each other properly. "Dead" halls do not give the acoustical "lift" necessary to the establishment of vocal contact between chorus members. This lack of vocal rapport is especially distressing when polyphonic music is performed.

TECHNICAL CAUSES

1 SUSTAINED LONG TONES may flat. While holding long tones, the chorister should always keep up the intensity level. The feeling of "drive" and "follow through" must always be present.
2 RELEASES, unless rhythmically precise and intensely (not loudly) vitalized, will often be accompanied by a slight drop in pitch. This is caused by failure to sustain the breath support for the full value of the note, or by anticipation of the release itself. All releases must be exact; executed on definite beats or their subdivisions.
3 SLURRING, SCOOPING OR APPROACHING NOTES FROM BELOW. Insistence on a mental and physical approach from *above* will eliminate this.

If a passage is still slurred in spite of the mental approach from above, practice the passage with a definite stop between each tone. When precision of pitch is attained, return again to the required legato.
4 ANTICIPATING THE PITCH OF THE NEXT NOTE and "sliding" into the pitch before the actual beat on which it is to be sung. Movement from note to note, except in certain cases of portamento and other special effects, must be made with "square corners". There should be no anticipatory curves which not only disturb individual "pitch centers" but also prevent the basic "group harmonic pitch center" from ever being established. One of the fundamental requirements for "ring" in a choral tone is the establishing of a group "in tuneness". Choirs with sloppy listening habits never establish this primary condition.
5 SOFT PASSAGES are sung flat because most singers do not intensify and vitalize their soft tones enough. This lack of mental and physical intensity not only results in a drop of pitch but also makes for a breathy, vitiated tone quality, lacking in vibrancy and lift.

To correct this condition, have the choristers sing their tones *loudly* and then repeat *softly* while retaining the same mental and physical sensations they experienced in producing the louder tones.
6 SLOW TEMPI will tend to cause flatting particularly when the group is immature and lacking in vocal control. It is a good interpretive as well as technical principle to retain "forward movement" in all slow compositions. Without this feeling of flow, tempi will become sluggish and static. A microscopic difference in speed may mean the difference between being in tune or out of tune.

Often the place of performance will influence the subtle choice of tempi. For instance in "dead" auditoriums, tempi must be picked up, whereas in "live" halls the sustaining characteristics of the hall will tolerate slower tempi.

| Approaching notes from the bottom: | Correction device — Mentally approach notes from above: |

7   REPEATED NOTES of a phrase are often wrongly approached from below, thus causing each succeeding note to be slightly lower in pitch. When singing repeated notes, think of each note as being higher than the one that preceeds it.

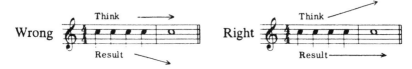

Another approach: Think of all the repeated notes as *one sustained* note.

8   FAULTY DICTION contributes to flatting. When pitch drops slightly, call for an intensification and vitalization of words. Whispering the text in an attempt to be heard in the distance will help. Exaggerated use of all muscles involved in word formation is recommended.

9   A GROUP WILL SOMETIMES ATTACK A SINGING CONSONANT BELOW THE PITCH OF THE FOLLOWING VOWEL and then slide up to the vowel pitch, or, even worse, pull down the vowel pitch to the level of the attacked consonant. The singing consonant must always be sung on the pitch of the following vowel. Particular attention should be paid to L's, M's, and N's.

10   "FOLLOWSHIP" is a contributor not only to faulty intonation but also to weaknesses in many other areas. Thinking ahead for *oneself*, rather than waiting for a neighbor or the group to establish the pitch, can correct this.

Use of the "spot check" on individuals, even for a few notes or measures, will keep choristers alert.

11   ATTACKING A NEW PHRASE BELOW THE PITCH LEVEL OF THE ONE IT FOLLOWS. Specific attention to "connecting links" (phrase endings to phrase beginnings) must be given if accuracy and flow between phrase units are to be preserved.

Also watch connecting links between modulatory passages and the old and new key areas. All too often the modulatory passage itself is carefully worked out, while the links are neglected.

12   A NEGLECTED BASS SECTION will flat a group. The leaps and skips common to a normal bass part should be executed clearly and sharply. An excellent device is to practice bass parts staccato or marcato.

13   CONTROLLED ABILITY TO FLAT OR SHARP SHOULD BE DEVELOPED. Practice deliberate sharping and flatting so that the piece will be a quarter to a half step sharp or flat at its conclusion. This raising or lowering of key should not be apparent as it progresses, but should occur so gradually as to be hardly discernible until a key check is made at the end. Deliberate flatting, while it may never be used, will be extremely servicable for those rare moments when the group, because of extreme tension, tends to sing sharp.

COMPOSITIONAL CAUSES

1 A COMPOSITION IS SOMETIMES WRITTEN IN A KEY WHICH MAKES SINGING IN TUNE DIFFICULT. Many well known choral selections are persistent trouble makers for all choral groups. Upon analysis you may find the following factors present which may contribute to the lowering of pitch:

  a) The vowels found in the text are predominantly IH (pit), EH (pet), and EE (me), sounds which most choir members control poorly.

  b) There will be many diphthong combinations which choir members abuse.

  c) The tessitura of one or more of the voice parts lies consistently in the high register.

  d) The tessitura of one or more parts lies consistently in "break" areas. The uncertainty of the amateur singer in negotiating the break (if present) often contributes to a loss of pitch control.

  e) Compositional flatting can often be remedied by *raising* the key of the selection a half or whole step.

2 INSECURITY OF THE INDIVIDUAL VOICE PARTS — "guessing" at the notes. A perpetual testing program, involving the hearing of your choristers in mixed quartets, will make them assume personal responsibility for the learning of individual parts.

3 SINGING A SUSTAINED NOTE AGAINST A MELODY LINE THAT IS DESCENDING. The sustained note will usually try to follow the downward movement of the descending part.

The mental concept of moving *upward* against the descending scale will correct this.

Knowledge of the relationship of the sustained note to the rest of the harmonic structure will also be helpful.

4 DO NOT CORRECT THE ENTIRE GROUP FOR FLATTING. Often just *one section* or *an individual* is at fault.

5 CONSISTENTLY HIGH OR CONSISTENTLY LOW RANGE, causing undue strains and pressures.

An occasional high or low note, if correctly approached, will not present any problem, but constant singing in tension areas is conducive to flatting.

6 ABRUPT AND VIOLENT CHANGES FROM *pp* TO *ff* and vice versa will affect pitch, not to mention quality.

SCALE AND INTERVAL CAUSES

1 THE FOLLOWING INTERVALS AND MELODIC PROGRESSIONS MAY CAUSE FLATTING:

  a) The fourth and fifth degrees of the minor scale.

  b) The third, sixth, and seventh steps of chords.

  c) The augmented step (six to seven) of the minor scale.

  d) Leading tones (particularly in inner parts.)

  e) The seventh scale step, particularly in a modulation.

f) Descending scale steps are usually too large. Descending intervals should be small and close to the tone above. The reverse is true of ascending scale steps.

g) Melodies that descend and suddenly turn upward.

h) Intervals that are repeated in sequence usually lose their proper interval relationship over a short period and tend to flat.

Compression of space will usually take place, particularly if the passage is a rapid one.

i) Three or more notes sung consecutively downward.

j) Whole tones are usually spaced too close together when ascending and too wide apart when descending. The same is true of semitones to an even greater degree. Devote some time to the singing of whole tone scales as well as chromatic scales. No piano is to be used.

2 MOST CADENCE POINTS ARE SIMPLE CHORDAL PROGRESSIONS (V - I, IV - I, etc.). These fundamental progressions should be practiced in different keys until the harmonic patterns are felt by the chorus members. An aural stability in these fundamental chord movements can contribute to the solution of the intonation problem.

3 PIECES IN MINOR KEYS, because of the nature of the sound, will tend to flat more frequently than those in major keys.

4 SUSPENSIONS normally are dissonant, resolving into a consonance. Groups invariably shy away from the dissonance and anticipate the consonant resolution. This timidity in sustaining the dissonance can only be eliminated by a firm and positive singing of the dissonance itself. The best procedure is to extract the dissonance and have the parts (usually 2) pointed out and sung in a vigorous fashion. After the shock of the dissonance is "enjoyed", practice the dissonance moving to the resolution. When this tension and ultimate relaxation between these vital points is fully appreciated, add the remaining parts.

COME, HOLY GHOST   J. S. Bach

CHAPTER 4

DYNAMICS

BASIC CONSIDERATIONS
and
DEVELOPMENT OF FUNDAMENTAL CONTROLS

The technical basis for most expression in music is the control of the *crescendo* and *decrescendo*. The intelligent and artistic application of a subtle *decrescendo*, a simple stress over a note or two, or a lengthy *crescendo* sweeping to an over-whelming climax is fundamental to the achievement of musical expression.

To gain facility in the handling of dynamic changes, the choir should, from time to time, spend a few minutes practicing the following exercises. In addition to bringing about fundamental control of dynamics, these technical drills increase awareness of the basic dynamic levels themselves.

ALL CHORUSES SHOULD HAVE VOCAL CONTROL OVER A MINIMUM OF SIX DYNAMIC LEVELS. These *relative* levels could be classified as *pp, p, mp, mf, f,* and *ff*. The *pp* could be defined as the softest possible tone a group can produce without excessive breathiness, loss of control, and wavering of pitch. The *ff* could be defined as the loudest possible tone that is in tune and is fully and richly produced without strain, stridency, or shouting.

To increase group control over dynamics, vocalize on long tones, either on unison pitches or on chord tones, using some, or all of the following exercises. Vowels preceded by consonants should be used (LAH, NEH, TEE, etc.) These are in

These are exercises in order of seeming difficulty:

a) *mf* < *f*

b) *mf* > *mp*

c) *mf* < *f* = *ff*

> *Mezzoforte* is the most desirable level to start with. It is easiest to produce a free tone at this level. Do not allow the choir to increase beyond a firm full *f*.
>
> Watch the quality of *ff*. Most choirs become "pushy" and raucous, substituting noise for broad, voluminous, velvety tone. Each chorister must be aware of *his individual peak* volume and know when he is "over the line" into the realm of noise. Work individually with those who do not know when they are "over the line", for these are the singers whose voices stick out, marring the blend of the group.

d) *mf* = *mp* — *p*

e) *mf* = *mp* = *p* — *pp*

> Watch the intensity level at *p* and *pp*. Most groups lose their body *intensity* and become sluggish as they sing softly. The exact opposite should be true in singing softly. Keep the intensity level as high or higher than when singing *f*. This *mental* and *physical* set will eliminate some of the breathiness that usually accompanies *pp* singing and will also keep the pitch from sagging.
>
> To secure a "spinning" *pp,* have the group sing a note or chord *ff* and then have them *repeat* it *pp* with the *identical body feel.*

f) *mf* < *f* > *mf*

Most groups readily master a straight crescendo and a reasonably controlled decrescendo, but their first experience with the *combination* of the two invariably results in a vocal sound that may be represented thus:

This "collapse" over the hump must be avoided by practising until a graceful, even curve of dynamic level is secured. Unless mastered in an isolated fashion, this valuable and almost indispensable dynamic idiom ($<$ $>$) can certainly not be applied to a note, a group of notes, or a phrase.

g) *mf* $>$ *mp* $<$ *mf*

Make certain that this is not executed: *mf* $>$ *mp* $<$ *f*

h) *mf* $<$ *ff* $>$ *mf*

i) *mf* $>$ *p* $<$ *mf*

j) *ff* $>$ *pp*

Watch that the *ff* is not strident, hard or over-sung.

Watch the intensity level at *pp*.

k) *pp* $<$ *ff*

Start firmly with good intensity. *Think loud.*

Practice these dynamic variations on individual long and short notes as well as on long and short arpeggio and scale exercises. Vary the vowel and dynamic

Vary the vowel, consonant and dynamic combinations. Try to devise exercises that relate to the compositions studied, as well as for purely technical purposes.

Scale Ex. [musical notation] Nah *p* $<$ *f* $>$ *p*   Arpeggio Ex. [musical notation] Nee. *f* $>$ $<$ *f*

Crescendi and *decrescendi* are rarely executed in so mechanical a fashion as outlined above, but these controls are necessary for complete technical mastery of the multiple combinations of dynamic ups and downs, sforzandos, stresses, etc., encountered in choral work.

A choir should also be capable of singing, at *any dynamic level*, a *straight* tone *without* deviation. This ability to maintain steady and unvarying pressure should be acquired parallel with the ability to control the subtleties of the *crescendo* and *decrescendo*. A well controlled, even tone contributes to the elimination of the common fault of *diminishing* toward the end of phrases or notes.

DEVICES FOR INCREASING CONTROL OF DYNAMICS:

a) Have one section make long or short *crescendi* and *diminuendi* while the other parts remain at one given dynamic level.

b) Have each section sing its part at a *different* dynamic level. For example, tenors sing *mf* while all others sing *pp;* or, sopranos and basses sing *p* while altos and tenors sing *f*, etc.

c) Give all choir members a mimeographed sheet of approximately fifty of the most commonly used musical terms, symbols, etc., (about half of these will apply to dynamics in some way) and instruct them to memorize them. Many choir members do not follow the indications of these symbols in the score because they *do not know their meaning.*

d) *All* indications in the score (*f, rit., pp, cresc.*, etc.) should be observed and adhered to until otherwise changed by the conductor. Most choir members observe only notes and words and need the suggestions that these other symbols be noted and correctly interpreted.

e) Sing through an entire piece at one dynamic level, *pp* for example. Relative to singing *pp,* the singers should be made aware of the fact that they *can be heard* when singing at this level. This feeling of not being heard, particularly in a large auditorium, has caused many singers to raise their dynamic level, substituting "earthly" *pianos* for "heavenly" *pianissimos.* Remember, if the individual can hear his own voice when singing softly, *he is singing too loud.*

TO ESTABLISH A FINE *pp* DO THE FOLLOWING:

1. Hum the passage. This establishes the standard of softness for a spinning *pp.*

2. Sing the passage in "hummy" style which means to sing words with a relatively closed mouth and to pronounce these words with very little movement of the articulatory organs. As the words are produced there should be a continuous feeling of hum and nasal resonance.

f) Sing succeeding phrases at different dynamic levels, getting louder or softer progressively.

Ex.: Phrase I — *pp,* Phrase II — *p,* Phrase III — *mp,* etc.

Ex.: Phrase I — *ff,* Phrase II — *f,* Phrase III — *mf,* etc.

g) Test the alertness of the choir members by a dynamic call-out game. This game simply consists in the calling out of new dynamic levels by the conductor as the choir is singing. The group is to sing at the called out level one beat after the level has been indicated and to continue at that level until the next call-out, which may take place at some convenient phrase point in the next measure or beat.

h) Sing a selection with the *opposite* markings of those indicated in the score. Awareness of these symbols is increased and a good bit of fun can be had by such a practice. (Dull Day Device.)

i) Have *one person* sing a given part with the *full choir* singing the other three parts. Thus an exercise, requiring, for example, *one* tenor to hold his part against a *full* chorus of soprano, alto, and bass parts, presents possibilities in training not only for *that tenor* but also for a choir which cannot bring its dynamic level down below *mf.* This particular weakness (*mf* singing) is the plague of most choral singing today.

DYNAMICS IN MUSICAL EXPRESSION

1 IN HOMOPHONIC MUSIC, DO NOT ALLOW ALL PARTS TO SING AT THE SAME DYNAMIC LEVEL, even though so indicated in the score. There is usually one part that should dominate. This part might have a melodic line, a counter melodic line, a chromatic alteration, an inner part that emphasizes a harmonic sweep or heightens the meaning of the text, etc. Only when the lines are in correct dynamic relationship do we have a condition that will contribute to good "balance".

2 KNOW THE DYNAMIC POTENTIAL AND LIMITATIONS OF YOUR GROUP. Do not *over extend* them on *ff* passages and conversely do not drive them to a dynamically lower level than their controls will allow. Only after these two extreme points of loud-

ness and softness have been established may the in-between levels be determined.

3 USE ONLY HALF OF YOUR CHOIR TO EXECUTE ETHEREAL PIANISSIMOS if your full choir is not able to achieve them. Caution: This is a *last resort*. It is better to instruct the choristers in the correct methods of securing the desired pianissimo.

4 USE ONLY PART OF YOUR CHOIR WHEN SINGING "UNDER" A SOLOIST. Again, this is an expedient device. Develop a fine soft "hummy" sound in your full choir.

5 EXPERIMENT BY TAKING AWAY PROM, OR ADDING VOICES TO GIVEN MEASURES, PHRASES AND SECTIONS. Interesting dynamic and tonal or color mass effects can be created by such experimentation. For example, if a sweeping dramatic crescendo is desired, it might be advisable to *start* the phrase with the "firsts" in every section, *gradually adding* the "seconds" at predetermined measures, until a surging sweep is attained. Similarly, one may wish a spinning, nebulous *pp*, in which case only the lighter voices are called upon to perform.

6 DO NOT ALWAYS MAKE A CRESCENDO ON AN ASCENDING PASSAGE. Conversely do not always execute a *decrescendo* on a descending passage. Many a lovely phrase can be turned by reversing this common tendency.

7 GAUGE THE APPROACH TO CLIMAXES CAREFULLY.

8 CRESCENDI AND DIMINUENDI WITHIN A PHRASE, A SECTION, OR A PIECE SHOULD NEVER BE OF THE SAME SIZE. They should vary in size and length according to the demands of text and music.

Mechanical and accordion-like surges should be avoided. Plan your surges in terms of intensity and amplitude. It is a rare instance where a succeeding series of crescendi and decrescendi is of the exact tonal dimension as the one it follows.

9 SUDDEN, ABRUPT CHANGES FROM LOUD TO SOFT AND VICE VERSA SHOULD BE MADE WITH GREAT DISCRETION.

10 EXTENDED CRESCENDI AND DECRESCENDI, SPREADING OVER SEVERAL PHRASES, RARELY GO STRAIGHT UP OR DOWN. Such crescendo effects are usually achieved by a series of smaller wave-like surges, gradually increasing and intensifying, giving the impression of being one massive sweep. Extended decrescendi are usually secured in the opposite manner.

11 ALL COMPOSITIONS WILL HAVE AT LEAST ONE MAJOR CLIMAX PLUS SEVERAL SECONDARY CLIMAXES leading to or away from these climax points. Climaxes are not always at the *fortissimo level*. Striking effects can often be secured by means of *pianissimo* climaxes.

While the major climax is usually obvious, the secondary climaxes are not quite so easy to discover or to plan in relation to it. Good musical expression is concerned with and dependent on establishing the relationship of these subordinate climaxes one to the other and then in turn to the major climax.

The conductor must plot and plan as best he can in order that logical, musically intelligent, and artistic results materialize. This "paper planning" with score in hand will be subject to modification as the selection is worked out with the chorus, but armed with this blueprint of dynamic indications, the conductor is one step ahead in his quest for true choral beauty.

Always make certain that the dynamic level of the phrase immediately preceeding the climax is not equal to or greater than that of the climax itself. Amateur singers (and some conductors) show considerable lack of restraint in such matters. The result is a let down at the climax, just when excitement, intensity, and volume should be at their greatest height.

12 A GENERAL CRESCENDO OR DECRESCENDO SHOULD BE MADE UNIFORMLY AND SI-

MULTANEOUSLY BY ALL SECTIONS. Too often one section "comes up" too soon or "drops down" too late. Sections not singing melody usually have the tendency to lag behind in their dynamic sweeps and recessions. This does not mean that imaginative and effective color waves cannot be created by experimenting in the "bringing up" or "bringing down" of one section before or after the others. This latter effect is the exception rather than the rule, however.

Relative to this, it might be well to point out that in order to secure more effective dynamic contrasts, there must be comparatively greater dynamic variation in the *lower* voice parts than in the *higher* ones.

13 IN THE INITIAL STAGES OF APPLYING DYNAMIC EFFECTS, EXAGGERATE THE SPECIFIC DYNAMIC LEVELS and/or crescendi and decrescendi. Thus a *mp* passage would be practiced *at first* at a *p* level, while a *mp* ⟍⟋ *mf* swell would be practiced *p* ⟍⟋ *f*. As soon as a definite control makes itself felt, subtleties are introduced and more delicate, as well as artistically more accurate dimensions are substituted.

14 DO NOT MERELY "SUSTAIN" A LONG NOTE. Keep "sending" it by use of some dynamic or intensity variation (crescendo, diminuendo, or a combination of both) during the course of the note. However, if another voice part has the melodic or harmonic interest, it must not be dominated by such a long note.

15 UP-BEATS MUST NOT DOMINATE (DYNAMICALLY) THE FUNDAMENTAL BEAT. These up-beat notes should be sung with the feeling of "going some place else."

16 HAVE YOUR GROUP PRACTICE SUBITO *p* AND *f* EFFECTS, *sfz's* AND THE LIKE.

17 DO NOT GIVE ALL BEATS EQUAL DYNAMIC EMPHASIS. The rules of rhythmic accent demand that the strong beats receive stress according to need and the weak beats be subordinated. This by no means suggests that a rhythmic thumping out of accented strong beats is to be encouraged, since this practice does not increase rhythmic vitality but merely results in metrical plodding.

Also, do *not add tone* to the naturally *accented beats* but rather *lighten* up on the *subordinate beats*. The result will be freedom, flow, and grace. The secondary beats will be stepping stones rather than places of rest. Forward flow, always desirable, will be the result.

18 ACCENTS AND STRESSES ARE OFTEN CREATED BY MEANS OTHER THAN DYNAMIC INTENSITY. These facts should be considered before any dynamic superimpositions are made:
  a) A long note placed among shorter notes will often sound emphasized.
  b) High notes give the impression of being accented when included among lower pitches.
  c) A skip from a low note to a high one will add dynamic emphasis to the high note.

19 DO NOT DISTORT OR FORCE THE TONE QUALITY WHEN SINGING ACCENTED NOTES.

20 VARY! DON'T JUST REPEAT. When you encounter a repetition of words, short motifs, phrases, rhythmic ideas, and the like, vary each repetition dynamically for purposes of variety and interest. Ascending imitation, for example, will usually call for greater intensity of tone. Other repeats call for less volume, more speed, less speed, etc. All these variations to be made within the bounds of good musical taste. Theatrical and artificially conceived effects are never appropriate.

I LOVE THEE
Edward Grieg

21 UNCALLED FOR ACCENTS WILL SOMETIMES OCCUR WHEN SHIFTING FROM A DARK VOWEL (AW) TO A BRIGHT VOWEL (E). Great care to make a smooth, fluid transition is in order here.

22 WHEN SKIPPING FROM A LOW NOTE TO A HIGHER NOTE, make certain that the higher note is not accented.

23 BE PARTICULARLY CAUTIOUS IN GIVING METRICAL ACCENTS IN PATTERNS OF SIX EIGHT NOTES.

Incorrect: Correct:

24 USE DYNAMIC VARIATIONS ACCORDING TO THE HISTORICAL PERIOD OF THE MUSIC. Music of the Romantic Period, for example, can be sung with more surging ebb and flow than the music of the Baroque Period, where bringing out the beauty of the part writing is the first consideration. In music of this last mentioned period, *f* and *p* were used in terms of contrast. Large crescendi and diminuendi, erratic tempo or emotional effects are inappropriate.

25 EACH ⎯◁ ▷⎯ MUST BE CONSIDERED IN RELATION NOT ONLY TO THE PHRASE BUT TO THE WHOLE PIECE AS WELL. Do not spoil an otherwise beautiful performance by indiscriminately bulging the dynamics out of proportion to the passage itself just because a composer has inserted a ⎯◁ ▷⎯ in the music.

Composer writes

Choir sings (incorrectly)

When no specific indication is given, the dynamic level should be raised *one* or, at the most, *two* degrees above the normal dynamic level of the particular phrase in which it occurs. For example, the aforementioned "A - men" passage will be tastefully executed *pp* < *p* > *pp* and not distorted to *pp* < *f* > *pp*.

26 *p* OR *f* ARE RELATIVE, NOT ABSOLUTE QUANTITIES. True, a *forte* should always have solidity and broadness, but a large volume of tone coming after complete silence or after a *pp* passage sounds much stronger than that same volume of sound succeeding a *mp* passage. The same dynamic relationships holds true in reverse.

27 ACCENTS SHOULD BE TREATED IN RELATION TO THE DYNAMIC LEVEL OF THE PHRASE WITHIN WHICH THEY OCCUR. For example, in a *pp* passage, the accent should be *small* compared with that same accent in a *ff* passage. Deliberation relative to the intensity, power and quality must be given these accents, since most composers use the *same signs* for *different accents*.

28 SYNCOPATION MUST BE EXECUTED AND SUSTAINED IN A FIRM MANNER. Keep in mind, however, that a syncopated note begins on a weak beat and is held across a strong beat. The emphasis on the strong beat is thereby neutralized.

29 USE THE "TIME ACCENT" FOR SPECIAL DRAMATIC EFFECTS. This consists of a building up of tremendous tonal power and intensity to a point beyond which it would seem that the group would find it impossible to go. When this point has been reached, the conductor *pauses* for a *brief moment* before giving the beat for the climactic note. This moment of silent suspension lends added impact, intensity, and excitement to the climax

30 DO NOT LET THE GROUP DIMINISH TOWARD THE END OF PHRASES. This is caused by:

    a) lack of breath,

    b) inertia,

    c) doubt as to where to cut off.

31 ALL VOICE PARTS ARE NOT EQUALLY IMPORTANT AT ALL TIMES. Bring out the voice parts that:

    a) have linear or melodic function,

    b) heighten harmonic color,

    c) have modulatory function,

    d) have imitative movement.

32 DO NOT LESSON THE DYNAMIC INTENSITY AFTER EACH NOTE IS ATTACKED. This is one of the chief factors that prevent the securing of a fine legato.

Dynamically we have this common picture [see *a*]:

If a good legato is to be obtained, the intensity level and "drive" must be retained and the dynamic level equalized from note to note [see *b*].

Any variation of dynamic intensity must be a deliberately planned one and not the result of mental and physical inertia.

CHAPTER **5**

TEMPO

ESTABLISHING A TEMPO

THE ESTABLISHING AND MAINTAINING OF THE CORRECT TEMPO IS ONE OF THE PRIMARY TASKS OF THE CONDUCTOR.

Factors to be considered in arriving at a proper tempo:

1 METRONOME MARKINGS: These are a *guide* to establishing the relatively correct speed. They are *approximate,* usually specifying a range of pace. Example: ♩ = 80 — 96.

Distinguish between metronome markings made by the composer and those that are editorial suggestions. Metronome markings may be used as a guide, but the following should be borne in mind:

    a) Metronomic indications by the composer are more valid, although it is generally known that composers are not always the best performers or conductors of their own works.

b) If you depart widely from the indicated tempo marks, have justifiable reasons for so doing.

2 TERMINOLOGY: Tempo indications (Allegro, Adagio, etc.) are *relative* and are subject to the influence of various considerations such as:

a) TEXT — The nature of the words has a direct bearing upon the matter of proper tempi. Mood, color, style and other characteristics of interpretation, which all have a relationship to tempi, are revealed through a study of the text. A conductor who is sensitive to the text as it exists in isolated fashion and as it relates to the character of its musical setting, will instinctively grasp the correct tempo.

Usually a text has one or many characteristics. It can be fanciful, humorous, morose, spiritual, etc., and, if the musical setting is a good one, text and setting will complement each other.

It should be noted that in a text are many key words and phrases that will sometimes lead the conductor into applying unwarranted stresses, exaggerated accelerandi and ritardandi, uncalled for tenuti, and other distortions of tempi or dynamics. Care should be taken when departing from a given tempo lest this "singing with expression" becomes a musically meaningless and utterly farcical experience. No conductor should make changes from an established tempo without adequate reason. This does not mean that strict tempi must be adhered to at all times. If a piece of music is to be fully revealed for what it is, it must be performed with fluidity and resiliency. This means *subtle* variation in tempo is a vital factor in well proportioned musical expression.

Tempo rubato, an extension and augmentation of this "flexible tempo", is to be used with circumspection lest it result in incongruous musical distortion. Good musical sense should prevail at all times. An axiom to adhere to is, "when in doubt, — *don't*".

b) EXECUTION OF TEXT — Another factor to be considered is the speed at which the text is to be rendered. If the words run together so as to become unintelligible, the tempo will have to be reduced in speed in order that clear enunciation of every word can take place.

3 ACCURACY OF NOTES: The overall tempo (particularly in faster movements) is sometimes arrived at by searching for the parts that have the most notes per beat and establishing the *maximum* speed at which all of these notes can be sung with clarity and precision.

4 SOMETIMES A COMPOSITION HAS SEVERAL TEMPI which are almost always in relation to and therefore dependent on each other. Hence, after establishing *one* tempo correctly, the others may be arrived at by deduction.

5 TEMPO VARIATIONS OF HISTORICAL PERIODS: Here a conductor's background, experience, and musical maturity stand him in good stead. Much listening, and association with music of all eras of musical history will assist him in establishing not only the tempi of music but also the style and other characteristics of different periods. For example, an Allegro in a composition by Bach will be slower than an Allegro in a piece by Mozart.

6 TRADITION: Here the instrumental conductor is at greater advantage since most of the works he conducts have, through their many performances, traditional aspects of interpretation applied to them, one of which is tempo. The choral director does

not have this aid (except in the case of major works) for he is constantly directing many, and oftimes recently published, shorter works that he has never heard
before either in concert or on record. He must fall back upon his own resources
to establish not only correct tempi, but other elements of interpretation as well.

7 MELODIC CHARACTERISTICS: The melodic character of the music is an invaluable
aid in arriving at a correct general tempo. The tempo must be slow enough to
bring out the full beauty of each part, but not so slow that a feeling of static
drag or a lack of forward movement is experienced.

8 HARMONIC CHARACTERISTICS: Pieces with frequent harmonic changes will usually
be sung slower than those with chords which do not change for several beats at
a time.

9 TEXTURE OF THE CHORAL PARTS: A crowded complicated score will invariably
be paced slower than one with less detail.

10 TEXTURE OF THE ACCOMPANIMENT: The fullness of the piano part will give a clue
as to the approximate speed of the work in question.

11 GROUP SIZE: This factor often has a bearing on choice of tempi. Invariably the
larger group will demand that slower tempi be adopted.

GENERAL PRINCIPLES

1 ALWAYS PRESERVE A "FLOW" OR FORWARD MOVEMENT REGARDLESS OF SPEED. A
choir with a mastery of rhythm and phrasing creates the impression of moving
more quickly than a choir whose actual pace is faster but whose rhythm is poor.

2 DO NOT SLOW DOWN WHEN CHANGING FROM MAJOR TO MINOR.

3 DO NOT GET FASTER IN ASCENDING PASSAGES or slow down on descending passages.

4 DO NOT SLOW DOWN WHEN SINGING SOFTLY.

5 DO NOT ACCELERATE ON LOUD PASSAGES.

6 DO NOT HURRY RAPIDLY MOVING PASSAGES, particularly those containing many even
notes unrelieved by notes of longer or shorter values. A strong rhythmic feel, combined with a sense of "hitting" and "stretching" *every* note, will eradicate this
problem. Aspirating each note will also slow down the group.

7 DO NOT "DRAG" SLOW PASSAGES. Create a feeling of forward movement to eliminate this tendency. Spot key words or notes and "move" to them. Do not "rest"
on these key words or notes, but touch them lightly, moving ahead at all times.

8 DO NOT GET FASTER WHEN MAKING A CRESCENDO.

9 DO NOT SLOW DOWN WHEN MAKING A DECRESCENDO.

10 DO NOT HURRY THE LAST BEAT OF ANY BAR.

11 DO NOT RUSH STACCATO PASSAGES. This tendency can be counteracted by putting
more "space" between each note.

12 YOUNG GROUPS SHOULD SING SLOW MUSIC SLIGHTLY FASTER THAN INDICATED, unless their ability to control nuances and sing sustained passages has been developed.

13 CAN YOU AND YOUR GROUP HOLD A STEADY BEAT? Try it against a metronome.

14 AFTER A RITARDANDO AND FERMATA, RETURN TO THE ORIGINAL TEMPO. Combat
the common tendency to return to a slightly *slower* tempo.

15 GIVE CORRECT PROPORTION TO THE BEATS AND THEIR SUBDIVISIONS IN YOUR RAL-
LENTANDO OR ACCELERANDO PASSAGES. The *longer* the rallentando *the more*

gradual the change of pace and vice versa.

Rallentandi and accelerandi are liable to become disorganized when each part has notes of different values. *The part that contains the shortest notes controls the speed.* All other parts must be aware of these short note "moving" parts.

16 DO NOT MAKE RALLENTANDI OR ACCELERANDI TOO SUDDEN OR TOO PRONOUNCED. All changes of speed should be made gradually.

17 DO NOT MAKE TEMPO CHANGES TOO GREAT. A useful rule is that the slackening or quickening of the tempo should never be more than double or half of the original pace. It should be pointed out, however, a change is rarely that great.

CHAPTER **6**

RHYTHM

1 MUST NOT BE SUNG , except in popular music.

2 MUST NOT BE SUNG unless so indicated by the nature of the phrase...

3 MUST NOT BE SUNG

4 SUSTAIN NOTES FULLY. must not become or

Relative to the values of notes, it would be well to point out that in $\frac{4}{4}$ time, for example, a quarter note is not finished until the second beat begins, a half note is not finished until the third beat begins, etc. *This robbing of values is one of the primary weaknesses in choral singing today.*

ONLY WHEN A CATCH BREATH IS TAKEN SHOULD A NOTE VALUE BE SHORTENED SLIGHTLY. In this case, shorten the value of the *last note previous to the breath*, execute the release, breathe rhythmically and sing the next note.

5 MAKE CHORISTERS AWARE OF NATURAL NOTE GROUP ACCENTS.

a) etc. Florid passages should be punctuated with *slight* rhythmic stresses to preserve the rhythmic swing.

Ex.:

and He shall pu - ri - fy _____

6 SYNCOPATED FIGURES AND IRREGULAR RHYTHMS SHOULD BE FIRMLY ATTACKED, em-, phasizing distinctly the divergence from the normal pattern. In syncopated passages, do not destroy the accent shift by placing stresses where they do not belong.

Ex.. must not be executed

7 Cross rhythms should be strongly emphasized so that they may stand out *against* each other.

8 DO NOT SING THROUGH RESTS. is not or

While rests are being given their full value, the group should maintain a feeling of flow and rhythmic drive during the rest period. Do not let down mentally, physically, or emotionally at a rest. Rests are as important a part of the music as are the notes.

O SACRUM CONVIVIUM

T. Tallis

9 RELEASES PRESENT NO PROBLEM WHEN ALL VOICES STOP SIMULTANEOUSLY. However, when there are releases on different beats for different voices, each voice

33

part must be given a specific beat (or part thereof) on which to release. Rhythmic chanting of words with overly vigorous releases will help here. This is particularly true in polyphonic music where the various voice lines end on different beats. These notes of varying length usually create the harmonic and rhythmic stresses and represent the endings of important phrase lines. If these releases are not properly planned for a certain beat or part thereof, the entire structure is devitalized.

CHAPTER 7

BLEND AND BALANCE

1 BEFORE ANY SINGLE VOCAL LINE CAN BE BLENDED INTO THE ENSEMBLE IT MUST BE A THOROUGHLY BLENDED UNIT IN ITSELF. Thus, if there are assertive voices in an alto section, they must first be brought into uniform balance within their *own section before* they can be blended with other sections. *Sectional blend* is *horizontal* with all voices going in the same direction rhythmically, with the same pitch, quality, quantity and tonal color. Once the various lines are blended horizontally, they may be merged with each other to form a combination of horizontal and vertical blend.

2 HEAVIER VOICES MUST NOT CRESCENDO TO THEIR FULLEST or else they will dominate others in the section.

3 LIGHT, LYRIC VOICES MUST NOT SING THEIR SOFTEST, for the bigger voices may not be able to diminish as much and will dominate.

4 DO NOT SHIFT QUALITY WHEN SINGING WIDE INTERVALS, either up or down. The change from lighter to heavier tone and vice versa may disturb blend and balance.

5 BALANCE YOUR GROUPS AROUND THE WEAKEST, NOT NECESSARILY THE SMALLEST SECTION. Balance depends on comparative resonance, power, and quality of the voices, not numbers.

6 IN SINGING POLYPHONIC MUSIC, make certain that the lower voices (basses and altos) have a fluid, buoyant quality, rather than a heavier tone.

7 BASIC TONAL BLEND IS ACHIEVED WHEN THE INDIVIDUAL TONAL CHARACTERISTICS OF EACH VOICE ARE FUSED INTO ONE SOUND.

Since the soft tone is nearest to a completely blended tone, it is advisable to start with this dynamic level. As more tone is added, individual qualities of certain voices will assert themselves. Choristers whose voices show bad qualities such as harshness, stridency, etc., should be cautioned to listen more carefully and adjust their production. Those having voices with desirable qualities, such as roundness and fullness, should be encouraged and the group sound centered around them.

8 COMPLETE BLEND IS POSSIBLE ONLY WHEN THE FOLLOWING PROPERTIES ARE PRESENT:

    a) Accuracy of pitch,
    b) Uniform vowels,
    c) Uniform dynamic level,
    d) Uniform tone color,
    e) Rhythmic unity,
    f) Uniform diction.

No blend is possible when the voices are pushed beyond their normal capacity.

9 DO NOT OVERLOOK THE SONORITY LEVEL OF VOICES especially at the extremes of their compass. Keep in mind the following:

    a) A high treble part is always prominent.

    b) High tenor notes dominate, not only because of pitch, but also because of their quality.

    c) Altos and basses do not come through when singing in the low ranges.

10 WHEN THE MELODY IS IN AN INNER PART, DO NOT BRING IT "UP" TO BE HEARD, bring the accompanying voices "down."

11 USE "TRAVELERS" FOR BALANCE. "Travelers" are selected members of each section who can shift to another voice part whenever necessary. Thus, when the melody is in the alto part, the first and second soprano "travelers" may be assigned to sing the alto part, the other sopranos singing their own written part. This adds weight where it belongs and takes weight from where it is not needed. In addition to balance, many varied "color" effects may be obtained by such manipulation of the voices. For example, tenors singing with the altos for greater depth; altos singing with the tenors for greater fluidity; altos singing a soprano part for added richness; sopranos singing the alto part to create a more lyric mood, etc.

12 WHEN FORMING SMALL ENSEMBLES, USE LIKE-TYPE VOICES IN EACH GROUP, as for instance, a group of "flute" voices or a group of "reed" voices. It is unwise to mix types in a small ensemble unless the members are musical and sensitive and have time to work out problems of blend and balance.

    In small ensembles, do not use voices with excessive tremolo (fast or slow). Do not confuse tremolo with vibrato, which is perfectly acceptable and in many cases desirable.

13 CLASSIFY YOUR VOICES INTO "FLUTE" (LIGHT), "REED" (REEDY), AND "STRING" (WELL BALANCED) VOICES. In seating these voices, alternate all three types: F R   S   F   R   S . This will assist in blending the sections.

14 BECAUSE OF CERTAIN PECULIARITIES, SOME VOICES BLEND ON HIGHER OR LOWER PARTS EVEN IF THEY DO NOT BLEND THROUGHOUT THEIR ENTIRE RANGE. If this is the case, transfer them to the section which will make use of that part of their vocal range that sounds well.

15 "SOLO" VOICES SHOULD BE MADE AWARE OF THEIR ARTISTIC RELATIONSHIP TO THE REST OF THE CHORUS and should not be allowed to dominate. To keep "strong" voices in line, surround them with light voices. The strong voices will tend to pull down their volume to match the dynamic level of the other voices.

    Heavier voices should usually be placed in the *rear* of the chorus because:

    a) If they are in the front, they frequently try to oppose the tonal mass coming at them from the rear.

    b) If in the rear, they will listen more carefully in order to keep themselves in balance with the group, and will thus reduce their natural volume.

    c) By being in the rear, their sound will be partially lost in the wings or absorbed by the bodies of the choristers in front of them, which will equalize their vocal output somewhat.

CHAPTER **8**

DICTION

SINGING DICTION SHOULD HAVE:

a) NATURALNESS — In listening to the text, the audience should not be aware of any foreign accent, affected mannerisms in pronunciation, or provincial or area dialects. Regional accents tend to disappear when proper concepts of vowel sounds are formed.

b) DISTINCTNESS — Every syllable, word and phrase must be clearly intelligible to the listener without giving the impression of stress or strain. A good deal of mental effort as well as a completely coordinated response of the articulatory organs must go into the performance if the results are to satisfy the listener.

When singing *legato,* do not overly exaggerate articulatory action to a point where this action disturbs the legato flow. In *legato* singing, particular attention must be paid to the jaw, which should move very *little* if a legato flow is to be preserved.

Actually the jaw has to move only for six letters (B, F, M, P, V, and W), and even in these instances the motions are small.

In legato style diction, emphasize the singing consonants L, M, N, NG, and R, bringing them up to the intensity level of the vowels. Thus the vowels and consonants are blended together and follow each other in an even stream of tone. The singer will have the feeling of "chewing the words".

With other consonants, use elision, by attaching the final consonant to the next word or syllable. This not only provides for a better legato, but insures more precision and unification in articulation.

In marcato diction, the opposite is true. Each note is an entity within itself, receiving a sharp accent and closing to the consonant quickly.

Staccato diction bears certain similarities to the marcato style, except that emphasis is placed on the rests or "space" between each note, rather than on the notes themselves.

c) NORMAL SYLLABIC ACCENT — Syllabic accent should be preserved as much as possible. Do not sing every syllable with equal strength, ignoring the normal inflection of the word. A good composer takes the relationship between word accent and metrical accent of the music into account and his music is so conceived that the two are in reasonably complete communion with each other.

Any work that calls for constant adjustment of these relationships is a poor one and should be dropped. This type of conflict is often present in compositions where translated texts are used.

d) KEY WORD EMPHASIS — Stressing, not to mention coloring, of key words within the phrase results in better text communication to the listener. By shaping the phrase with due consideration of the fact that not all words or syllables are equally important, we find that this shifting of weights and stresses on words makes the text more meaningful. Do not distort musical lines or resort to tasteless exaggeration, however.

CHAPTER 9

VOWELS

GENERAL PRINCIPLES

1 WHEN SINGING A WORD BEGINNING WITH A VOWEL, AVOID MAKING AN INTRODUCTORY SOUND IN THE THROAT. This objectionable *glottis stroke* is caused by the coming together of the vocal chords *before* the start of a tone.

2 VOWEL SOUNDS MUST REMAIN THE SAME FROM BEGINNING TO END AND SHOULD NOT CHANGE IN ANY WAY. Example: A sustained "AH" must not close into "UH." This vowel modification is particularly noticeable when singing softly or when singing the same vowel on a long florid passage.

The chorister is often in doubt as to the actual vowel of a word or syllable. Each word or syllable should have its specific vowel isolated.

Example: Glory to God
AW IH OO AH

The vowel mold is to be retained for its full rhythmic value, moving decisively to the next vowel mold at the proper moment. Positive thinking, relative to the actual vowel sound, will bring about a physical response resulting in the correct vowel mold and not an *approximation* of it.

In the case of diphthongs, ignore the *vanishes* completely. They can be easily inserted at the proper time.

3 SHAPE THE MOUTH FOR THE VOWEL, not for the consonant. This shaping must take place *as* the breath is taken, not *after* the breath is taken.

4 CERTAIN VOWEL SOUNDS MAY BE MODIFIED to improve the tone quality (particularly on high notes), but they should not be altered into a totally unrecognizable form.

5 VOWELS THAT ARE NOT UNIFORMLY PRODUCED by *all* members of the group will not only disturb the quality of the group tone and blend, but will also affect the clarity of the *diction*. A mixture of bright, dark and open vowels, coming from different individuals, will result in a medley of tone color that will tend to make words less understandable.

6 WATCH THOSE "LEISURELY SINGERS". They take too much time to move through vowels and consonants. These drawling, slow movers should be taught to move lips and tongue with snap and precision.

7 USE ALL VOWELS IN VOCALIZING. This includes all modifications of the cardinal vowels. Do not neglect diphthong combinations.

8 WHEN TWO FORMS OF ANY VOWEL ARE ACCEPTABLE, USE THE BROADER FORM FOR SINGING.

9 WHEN IN DOUBT ABOUT THE EXACT PRONUNCIATION OF A VOWEL, CONSULT A DICTIONARY.

PRIMARY VOWELS
and
RELATED SOUNDS

A as in *Father* — Keep the jaw dropped and mouth open (at least the width of the thumb). The tongue lies easily in the bottom of the mouth, the tip in light contact with the lower front teeth. The arch of the mouth is high and broad. Avoid singing the AH *back* in the mouth lest a throaty AW sound be heard.

If AH tends to be too "throaty", the following exercises will help to bring it forward:

EE_AH_EE_AH_EE, EE_AH_EE_AH_EE, EE_AH_EE_AH_EE, EE_AH_EE_AH_EE,
ING_AH_ING_AH_ING, ING_AH_ING_AH_ING, ING_AH_ING_AH_ING, ING_AH_ING_AH_ING,

EE_AH_EE_AH_EE EE_AH_EE_AH_EE, EE_AH_EE_AH_EE, EE_AH_EE_AH_EE.
ING_AH_ING_AH_ING, ING_AH_ING_AH_ING, ING_AH_ING_AH_ING, ING_AH_ING_AH_ING.

The forward feeling of the EE or ING should be *retained* when singing the AH. In this way, proper resonance is secured and the forward sensation of the EE being carried into the AH gives it the "ring" it needs for proper projection.

In this, as well as subsequent exercises, the transition from one vowel to the other should be made with *great smoothness*. This "carrying glide" will blend the desirable characteristics of one vowel into the other. This carrying glide is indicated by the ‿

Watch those who add an R (*ahr*). This is a characteristic of speech in certain parts of our country. Incidentally, deliberate vocalization on AHR is helpful in eliminating the tendency in *male* voices to color their vowels with a throaty UH. When vocalizing on AHR roll the R slightly. This encourages a high palate position and brightens the vowel sound.

A as in *Ask* or *Add* — Usually too nasal. Modify slightly by practicing the broad A (*father*) and working back until a fuller A (*ask*) sound is heard. Do not sing "AHSK", however.

A as in *Paw* — Keep this vowel forward. Do not use this as a substitute for AH unless the AH is thin and nasal. Excellent for developing fullness of voice and darkness of color. Avoid over use of this vowel lest an excessively covered sound develops. This vowel is usually lacking in vibrancy and ring.

A as in *Fate* — Usually sounds "teethy" and edgy. Treat this as a *diphthong* combination. Sustain it on an EH (*pet*) sound and vanish on an EE (*me*) or IH (*hit*).

Fate
FEH ‿ EET
1 2 3 4

E as in *He* — Tends to be too harsh and "teethy". This vowel should be sung dark. Round the lips as if singing OO (*moon*), then superimpose the EE (*he*) on this mold. The result should be equivalent to the French "*u*" or the German umlaut "*ü*". Avoid tension in jaws and the clenching of teeth. The following exercises will be helpful in establishing roundness on an EE:

OO_EE_OO_EE_OO,   OO_EE_OO_EE_OO,   OO_EE_OO_EE_OO,   OO_EE_OO_EE_OO,

OO_EE_OO_EE_OO,   OO_EE_OO_EE_OO,   OO_EE_OO_EE_OO,   OO_EE_OO_EE_OO.

Keep lips rounded on the EE. Do not draw the lips back against the teeth. When properly focused and resonated, EE is excellent for acquiring ring and vitality as well as for brightening "thick", "yawny" voices. The following will be helpful:

VEE VEE VEE VEE,   VEE VEE VEE VEE,   VEE VEE VEE VEE,   VEE VEE VEE VEE.
NEE NEE NEE NEE,   NEE NEE NEE NEE,   NEE NEE NEE NEE,   NEE NEE NEE NEE.
MEE MEE MEE MEE,   MEE MEE MEE MEE,   MEE MEE MEE MEE, MEE MEE MEE MEE.

E as in *End* — Tends to be strident. To mellow this vowel, practice the following:

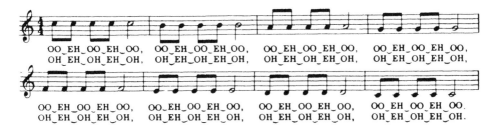

OO_EH_OO_EH_OO,   OO_EH_OO_EH_OO,   OO_EH_OO_EH_OO,   OO_EH_OO_EH_OO,
OH_EH_OH_EH_OH,   OH_EH_OH_EH_OH,   OH_EH_OH_EH_OH,   OH_EH_OH_EH_OH,

OO_EH_OO_EH_OO,   OO_EH_OO_EH_OO,   OO_EH_OO_EH_OO,   OO_EH_OO_EH_OO.
OH_EH_OH_EH_OH,   OH_EH_OH_EH_OH,   OH_EH_OH_EH_OH,   OH_EH_OH_EH_OH.

Watch careless modifications, particularly when this vowel occurs on an unstressed syllable.

> Example: "seven" becoming "sevin" or "sevuhn",
> "roses" becoming "rosuz" or "rosiz",
> "misses" becoming "missiz" or "missuhs",
> "anthem" becoming "anthum" or "anthihm".

I as in *Hit* — For added depth and richness, color this vowel with a bit of EE (*me*). Do not sing "heet", however. Do not draw the lips back against the teeth, keep them well rounded so that a sound of greater depth is produced.

This vowel must be watched when it is on an *unstressed* syllable.

> Example: "Spirit" becoming "spirut" or "spireht".

O as in *Vote* — Not too troublesome because of its central placement. The tongue lies easily in the bottom of the mouth, the tip touching lightly against the lower front teeth. This is a diphthong combination *sustaining* on OH and *vanishing* on OO.

Keep a bit of the AH color when singing OH. Set the AH mold and adjust lips to pronounce OH.

Do not substitute the UH (*but*) sound for OH.

O as in *Cot* — Sometimes pronounced too brightly, for ex. CAHT.

O as in *Lord* — Must have an "awe" sound. Do not swallow.

OO as in *Soon* — An easy vowel to produce. Lips, well rounded, with a cavernous feeling inside the mouth will usually produce a good OO sound.

Too much vocalization on an OO sound will result in a hooty quality. Balance its use with other vowels.

It is practically impossible to produce this sound poorly and, if the basic sound of any group is rough or strident, vocalization on this vowel will help to eliminate the roughness.

If this vowel should be throaty, practice by forming it on an O (*note*) mold, slowly changing to OO (*soon*).

Preceding OO (*soon*) with an EE (*me*) will also help to take some of the throatiness out.

Watch the tendency to diphthongize this OO sound as a result of failure to bring the back of the tongue quickly to the right position. The result of this lethargic action is a *drawl. DO* becomes *DEEOO*, etc.

UH as in *Up* — Tongue should lie flat, jaw moderately dropped. Do not get throaty. Watch for curling of the tongue and tightening of the base of the tongue. Use AH (*father*) as the basic vowel mold, modifying it into UH. Practice this exercise with as little shift from AH as possible. This will help prevent the throaty tendency. The EE — UH exercise is also effective in preventing throatiness.

CHAPTER **10**

CONSONANTS

1 CONSONANTS ARE INTERRUPTIVES, as contrasted with vowels, which are sustaining elements. In view of these opposing functions, the consonant must be executed sharply, with great definition and clarity, consuming as little time in its execution as is possible.

The only exceptions to this are such voiced sounds as L, M, N, etc., which should be lingered upon briefly as an aid in establishing continuity of vocal line. These consonants must not be given the full value of a vowel, however, nor must they be sustained in ludicrous fashion as is so often heard.

2 ALL MUSCULAR ACTIVITY OF THE LIPS, TONGUE, AND OTHER ARTICULATING ORGANS MUST BE GREATLY EXAGGERATED TO MAKE WORDS INTELLIGIBLE. This is particularly true when singing in large halls. Muscular activity that is adequate for conversation is inadequate for singing. However, do not exaggerate this action to a point where muscles become tired and stiff, thus losing their resiliency and flexibility.

3 WHEN A VOWEL FOLLOWS A CONSONANT, HAVE THE TONGUE ASSUME THE CORRECT POSITION FOR THE VOWEL as soon as the consonant is released.

4 SING VOICED CONSONANTS AT THE PITCH LEVEL OF THE VOWELS.

Wrong ... Right ...

m–ee   m–ee

5 DO NOT STOP THE TONE AS CONSONANTS AND VOWELS ARE FORMED. Press the tone *through* the consonant, letting the vowel spring forth after a *quick* execution of the consonant.

6 WHEN TWO CONSONANTS FOLLOW EACH OTHER, INTRODUCE A VERY BRIEF EXTRA SYLLABLE, IH or UH, to give definition to the consonants as well as a carrying quality to the phrase.

Example: "God loved" is sung Gah *di* luhvd *ih* or Gah *du* luhvd *uh.*

This added sound must be extremely *brief* and *delicate* otherwise it will become distorted and in bad taste.

7 DO NOT SING THE CONSONANT ON THE PREVIOUS NOTE, particularly in ascending passages. This is a very common practice.

8 BEWARE OF THE "M" THAT OFTEN SOUNDS BEFORE A CONSONANT WITHOUT THE SINGER REALIZING IT. This usually occurs on the first note of a piece.
Ex.: "M" God.

9 USE ALL CONSONANTS AS PREFIXES WHEN VOCALIZING YOUR GROUPS. Each consonant has a distinct use as well as a problem of execution. Good articulation of consonants is dependent on their regular and systematic practice and should not be neglected because of emphasis on vowel work.

10 WATCH FOR "SOUND OMISSIONS" IN SPEECH.
"reck-a-nize" instead of "rec-og-nize", "li-ba-ry" instead of "li-bra-ry," etc.
Also watch for *"sound additions"*
"ath-a-le-tics" instead of "ath-let-ics", "fil-lum" instead of "film," etc.

11 FOR ADDITIONAL CLARITY, RELEASE ALL FINAL CONSONANTS WITH A VOCALIZED, ADDED "IH".

Example:

The IH sound must be very short and not modified into a heavy UH or AH sound.

12 OVER-ARTICULATION, THE OPPOSITE OF CARELESS ARTICULATION, IS SOMETIMES PRESENT. In this case the consonants are so exaggerated as to cause lack of flow and loss of tone length. This is a weakness, for the group must be able to combine decisive, percussive consonants without interrupting the flow of a legato vocal line.

13 CHORISTERS SHOULD NOT BE ALLOWED TO SING AS THEY SPEAK. Slovenly speech habits (indistinctness, slurring, consonant omissions, etc.) acquired in ordinary conversation is thoroughly inadequate for singing.

Most people understand each other in conversation because of context. The conversationalists, hearing a few key words or syllables, instinctively fill in by mentally supplying the proper word or phrase. However, when words are *sung,* the length of note values and the resultant sustaining of syllables make this "guessing" at words less possible.

14 THE CONDUCTOR SHOULD NOT DECEIVE HIMSELF BY THINKING HE HEARS WORDS WHEN HE DOES NOT. Being familiar with the text, he allows defective diction to pass as being understandable to an audience, when in reality it is not.

SPECIFIC CONSIDERATIONS

1 B as in *Bee* — Formed by an explosive parting of the lips. Do not use too much breath in its execution nor explode as vigorously as in executing a P. Have no undue jaw movement.

2 C as in *Face* — A soft "s" sound. Do not anticipate or sustain the hiss.

3 D as in *God* — The tip of the tongue is placed in light contact against the *gum ridge* (the bump or ridge above the teeth) and sharply snapped from this position. Do not press the front of the tongue against the place where teeth and gum meet. Contrast D sharply with T.

4 F as in *Fad* — Formed by sharply snapping the lower lip from under the upper teeth. Contrast F sharply with V since production is the same.

5 G as in *Flag* — A guttural sound. Do not use too much breath to make it. Always sing lightly so as not to fatigue the throat muscles. Do not use this often as a prefixed consonant in vocalizing lest tensions develop.

6 H as in *Hard* — An aspirate. Useful in singing passages in which several tones are assigned to a syllable. The insertion of an H between every note serves to detach the notes, giving them definition and eliminating the slurring tendency.

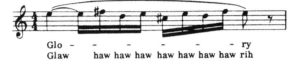

Glo - - - - - - ry
Glaw   haw haw haw haw haw haw rih

When aspirating, watch that no undue loss of breath occurs. Give a sharp, crisp edge to each note.

A lazy diaphragm is responsible for a dropped H. A solid, percussive action from the diaphragm will remedy this problem.

7 J as in *Jam* — No problem.

8 K as in *Klan* — See "G" as in Flag.

9 L as in *Lad* — Do not pronounce this too far back in the throat. The tongue tip should be lightly pressed against the upper teeth ridge and the back of the tongue not unduly raised.

Use only the smallest edge of the tongue tip, otherwise heaviness will result.

The L is a voiced consonant and may be sustained. It should be given time to be heard. Do not prolong it as you would a vowel, however.

Do not *anticipate* a final L in words. The integrity of the main vowel will be destroyed if the tongue gradually moves toward the roof of the mouth. The tongue should remain down until the very last moment before the sounding of the L.

Wrong: Right:

Faw - aw - l - l   Faw aw aw awl
1 & 2 & 3 &4&   1 & 2 & 3 & 4 &

Do not omit the L, as "aw right" for "all right".

10 M, N — Voiced consonants. Excellent for sustaining legato style. Avoid the tendency to pinch these sounds. They should be sung lightly and freely.

A device ior securing a resonant M or N is to sing the vowel OH and then close the lips and teeth around this vowel, thereby producing a free hum.

When singing M's and N's increase the intensity level to a point past that of the preceding vowel so that the M's and N's are heard. When moving to the following vowel, drop the intensity level, otherwise the vowel will "explode" out of all dynamic proportions.

Example:

I'm   com - ing.
Ah eem   kuhm m   ee   ee   ng
3   &   1   &   2 &3   &
-     +   -   +   -   -   +

at + increase intensity
at - decrease

43

M's and N's should be given time to "sound" but they must not be given the length of a vowel or prolonged in cheap and incorrect imitation of so called "radio style".

M's and N's must be sung on the pitch of the vowel.

M's and N's are good consonantal prefixes for bringing forward resonance into the tone. Do not use exclusively, however, or nasality may develop.

11 NG as in *Sing* — All remarks made with reference to M and N apply here.

Sing ING with EE color (EENG), not IHNG or EHNG.

This sound is excellent for developing forward resonance.

Exercises on ING and ÜNG performed with two fingers between the teeth help to release jaw tensions. These sounds serve to introduce "cover" sensation or postnasal resonance. The male singer must utilize "cover" on his upper notes to prevent a "shouty", open quality from coming in.

12 P as is *Pop* — Pronounce this vigorously with the lips. Differentiate from B. Use P and B as prefixed consonants to wake up lazy lips. Keep the jaw relaxed since movement of the lips does not necessarily mean a movement of the jaw.

13 Q as in *Queer* — No problems.

14 R as in *Rod* — Do not pronounce this in the throat.

Over-rolling an R is as bad as under-articulating it.

When an R comes at the beginning of a word, it may be strongly rolled.

A roll of an R *before* another consonant, such as in "start", is to be a short flip.

If a word syllable needs emphasis, an R may have three or more rolls.

Never (well, hardly ever) roll a *final* R.

Do not close into the R when singing a sustained note. Sustain on the vowel until the exact moment of closure to the consonant. This anticipation of the "R" sound is known as burring.

When an R comes between two vowel sounds, pronounce it with the *second* syllable. "Bury" becomes *beh-ree*, not "behr-ee".

Southerners have a tendency to omit the R altogether. This is a defect that should be eliminated.

15 S — This sibilant is an irritating and unmusical sound when prolonged excessively or produced without control. Never sustain this sound. Hold the vowel and touch the S lightly at the last possible moment. Most singers close into the S too soon and hold their tongue against the roof of the mouth too long. Drop the tongue to the floor of the mouth quickly to cut off the S.

To minimize S sounds:

1. Have part of the chorus *lisp* the sibilant.
2. Have part of the group omit it entirely.

If an S occurs between syllables, pronounce it with the *second* syllable. Example: "la-sting", not *las-ting* or *last-ing.*

If the S comes at the beginning of a word, pass to the vowel as rapidly and lightly as possible.

When two S's come together, *eliminate* one. Example: "this seat" becomes *thi' seat.*

16 T as in *Tip* — Touch only the tip, not the whole front of the tongue, to the *gum ridge* and execute as in D. Differentiate between T and D.

Watch T, particularly in the *middle* of a word, for it often becomes D. (Metal — *medal*, water — *wader*.)

Watch such sound substitutions as "meetchew" for "meet you", etc.

17 TH as in *Earth* — Do not prolong the TH sound. Sharp action of the tongue with very little loss of air is the key.

18 V as in *Vine* — Distinguish between this and F.

19 W as in What — All words spelled WH sound an H first.

Example: "What" becomes *hwaht*, not *waht*.

As an initial consonant, insert a quick OO (*moon*) before it.

Example: *oowonderful*.

20 X — No problems except for excessive sibilance.

21 Y as in *Yes* — No problems. Excellent consonant for loosening the jaw. *(Yah, Yoh, Yoo, Yee, Yeh, etc.)*

Do not insert a Y between two unlike vowel sounds.

Example: the (y) arm.

22 Z as in *Zoo* — See S.

CHAPTER **11**

DIPHTHONGS

GENERAL PRINCIPLES

1 IN SINGING, EACH SYLLABLE MUST HAVE ONLY "ONE BASIC" VOWEL SOUND. In the case of diphthongs, where two vowel sounds exist, only one of these vowels can be basic (fundamental). The other secondary vowel (vanish) must be treated as a consonant and clipped off crisply and precisely. This rule applies whether the diphthong is sung on one note or many notes.

2 DO NOT SHIFT VOWELS "GRADUALLY" ON A SUSTAINED DIPHTHONG. All "vanishes" must be treated as consonants and movement to them made quickly. Anticipating the "vanish" and moving into it before its proper beat will destroy blend and vowel unanimity because choristers will be at different stages of vowel closure and will be singing slightly different vowel sounds as they gradually approach the vanish. To correct this, simply indicate a definite beat or part thereof on which to release the "vanish" crisply.

This unanimity of vowel sound is as important as unanimity of pitch. There is no more valid reason for accepting several different vowels or vowel modifications than there is for accepting slightly different pitches from the group.

3 THE PITCH OF THE "VANISH" MUST BE THE SAME AS THAT OF THE FUNDAMENTAL VOWEL SOUND.

BASIC DIPHTONGS

I as in *Night* — consists of the fundamental AH (*father*), which is sustained for almost the entire length of the tone, and the vanish EE (*me*) or IH (*pit*), which is sounded just before the tone is ended.

Example: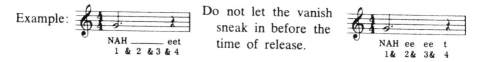

Do not let the vanish sneak in before the time of release.

NAH _____ eet
1 & 2 & 3 & 4

NAH ee ee t
1& 2& 3& 4

This sound combination is not always spelled with an I. For example *eye, justify, etc.*

OI as in *Toil* — consists of a fundamental AW (*awe*) sustained and a vanish EE (*me*) or IH (*pit*).

Example:  Watch that vanish!

TAW _____ eel
1 & 2 & 3 & 4

OY as in *Boy* — consists of a fundamental AW (*awe*) and a vanish EE (*me*). or IH (*pit*).

BAW _____ ee
1 & 2 & 3 & 4

OU as in *Out* or OW as in *Now* — consists of a fundamental AH (*father*) and a vanish OO (*moon*).

AH _____ oo t
NAH _____ oo
1 & 2 & 3 & 4

A as in *Pay* — consists of a fundamental EH (*pet*) and a vanish EE (*me*) IH (*pit*).

PEH _____ ee
1 & 2 & 3 & 4

OH as in *Slow* — consists of a fundamental OH (*go*) and a vanish OO (*moon*).

Sloh _____ oo
1 & 2 & 3 & 4

E as in *New* — Here the vanish *precedes* the fundamental and consists of a vanish EE (*me*) and a fundamental OO (*moon*).

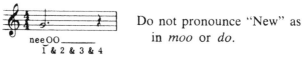

Do not pronounce "New" as in *moo* or *do*.

neeOO _____
1 & 2 & 3 & 4

46

CHAPTER **12**

TONE COLOR

SINGERS AND THE DIRECTOR MUST DEVELOP IMAGINATIVE USE OF VOCAL TONE COLOR IF COMPLETE EXPRESSION IS TO BE ACHIEVED AND THE FULL SIGNIFICANCE OF THE WORDS AND MUSIC TO BE COMMUNICATED TO THE LISTENER.

All voices have multitudinous shades of vocal tone color that can be utilized in executing a musical phrase. Appropriate tone color exists when the quality and character of the voice emotionally reflects the sentiment of the words and the expressiveness of the music.

Whether singing or speaking, the words "I hate you" and "I love you" will sound quite differently if they are projected with meaning colored by the thought and feeling behind those words.

All emotions have appropriate tone color and it is the duty of the conductor to stimulate an imaginative response to the emotional content of words and music. A choir, singing without a grasp of verbal beauty or conviction, is a colorless choir at best.

Tone color response may be developed as follows:

1 ELICIT A PHYSICAL RESPONSE TO THE MUSIC. This is reflected in body attitudes and facial expression which affect tone color. Tone color in turn contributes toward mood and the projection of mood to the listener.

Choristers must be freed from their inhibitions and conditioned to "letting themselves go". The amateur is always fearful of "looking foolish" and the removal of this stumbling block to emotion and mood is the first hurdle the conductor must negotiate.

Emotional thought translated into muscular action is a cardinal principle to be learned by a chorister. Even the taking of breath must be initiated by the emotional thought behind it. In fact, the first phrase begins, not with the first note, but with the breath previous to it.

In brief, "look like the music". This applies to the director as well as to the singer. For the conductor must always be the dramatist revealing, through face and body, the inner emotion he feels.

2 ELICIT AN EMOTIONAL RESPONSE BY AN ANALYSIS OF THE TEXT. This can be achieved by:

   a) A good, sensitive recitation of the text by the conductor or a member of the group.

   b) Discussion of the mood of the text. What does it express? What emotion should be conveyed to the audience?

   c) Highlighting key words and phrases that are emotionally expressive (*cold, hate, despised, loving,* etc.), reciting them feelingly and carrying this expression into the singing. Group these key words and phrases together and shape this word line into a *phrase*, bringing out the important words by giving them more dynamic weight than the unimportant connective words. The singing of *phrases* is a basic requirement for good interpretation and without this "phrase arch" the music becomes shapeless and devoid of meaning.

    d) Suggest that the choir members join choric speaking groups. Participation in activities such as these will teach them projection, proper timing, good speech habits, tone coloring, text analysis, etc. Develop an actor's concept of words in order to portray deeper emotional sense.

3 ELICIT AN EMOTIONAL RESPONSE BY AN ANALYSIS OF THE MUSIC. Point out ways the composer has brought out the meaning of the text by use of harmonic and instrumental color, rhythmic patterns, imagery, contrapuntal devices, and other musical ideas. This will make the composition more meaningful to the performer.

All these factors contribute to the development of a subjective tone color capable of conveying emotional and spiritual attitudes to the audience.

CHAPTER **13**

STAGING

1 USE SIMPLE LIGHTING EFFECTS from the front, side, or behind the group. Changes of color and light intensity can augment a mood.

2 REGROUP THE CHORUS FROM TIME TO TIME.

3 USE A CHANGE OF DRESS OR COSTUME. Even a simple change from choir robes to evening gowns and dark suits after the intermission is effective.

4 USE CHOREOGRAPHY to highlight choral selections. A group of three contrasting songs, for example, could be "staged" by the physical education department or by a student in your own group. A local dancing instructor will usually cooperate.

5 USE "BUSINESS" IMPLIED BY THE SONGS. This is probably best for the novelties or humorous songs that should be included for program balance.

6 USE SIMPLE BACK DROPS, decorative pieces pinned on curtains, or simple sets which can be constructed by the art department or by your own group.

7 USE A SCENE FROM AN OPERA OR OPERETTA for either half of your choral concert. Greater program interest and variety can thus be secured.

CHAPTER **14**

CRITERIA FOR SELECTION OF CHORAL MUSIC

1 TEXT
    a) Does it have literary value?
    b) Are the words easy to sing?
    c) If a translation, is it a good one?

2 MUSIC
    a) Is it original in concept?

b) Is it melodically, harmonically, and rhythmically interesting?

c) Is its appeal lasting, or is it spontaneous but ephemeral?

d) Is the musical setting in keeping with the style and mood of the text?

e) Do the basic ideas develop and grow into an organic whole, or are they episodic, bearing no vital relationship to each other?

f) Is the part writing vocal rather than instrumental?

g) In the case of an arrangement; is it in keeping with the spirit of the song or is it over-arranged?

h) Are the ranges suitable? Are matters of tessitura taken into consideration?

i) Are the vocal lines interesting?

j) Will it appeal to both performers and audience?

k) Is it worth the effort necessary to prepare it for public performance?

l) Does the work fit into a balanced repertoire?

m) Is it within the ability of the group to learn without excessive difficulty?

n) Can its meaning be understood by the group so that a mature, emotional performance can result?

o) If accompanied, does the piano enhance the vocal parts or does it detract because it is over-elaborate and showy?

3 GENERAL CONSIDERATIONS

a) Do not underestimate your group. Select works that are challenging.

b) Vary the categories of selections in your repertoire. Do not neglect contemporary works.

c) Sing both accompanied and unaccompanied compositions.

d) Know the weaknesses and strengths of your organization and learn to recognize music that will show it to advantage.

e) Use valid editions only.

f) Be judicious in using standard works rearranged for voice combinations other than those for which they were originally scored.

g) Instrumental works arranged for chorus with texts (which are often bad) are to be avoided.

h) Build a personal library of single octavos and refer to it often.

CHAPTER **15**

AUDIO AIDS

1 USE A TAPE RECORDER AT REHEARSALS TO CHECK YOURSELF. Look for the following:

a) Are your directions clearly given?

b) Do improvements really take place with each repetition or are the improvements imagined?

c) Do you talk too much — without purpose?

d) Are there too many "dead spots" — dull pauses while the group waits for the *conductor* to decide when he is going or what he is to do next. Usually accompanied by the scratching of the head, the stroking of the chin and the "hms", "wells", "ahh's" and other vocal musings of the doubtful.

The conductor must know his return point or next direction to the group *before* he stops.

2 RECORD YOUR GROUP EARLY IN THE SEASON and compare this performance with subsequent recordings made at three month intervals. Point out any areas of improvement. This will contribute to the morale of your group, since they are not really conscious of the gradual improvement that takes place from month to month.

3 KEEP TAPES OF ALL CONCERTS AND IMPORTANT PUBLIC APPEARANCES. Record outstanding soloists and ensembles to assemble a "Choral History" of your school or church group.

4 RECORD OTHER GROUPS AS WELL AS YOUR OWN AT CONTESTS. Valuable teaching points, both positive and negative, can be found by listening analytically to other groups. In addition, many fine choral selections, not available on commercial records, may be preserved for future reference.

5 RECORD AMATEUR OR PROFESSIONAL GROUPS who visit your area or perform in your school.

6 RECORD GROUPS ON RADIO OR TELEVISION. This can be particularly valuable at holiday seasons. However, whenever you use your tape recorder be sure you have secured permissions from the necessary sources.

7 AT CONFERENCES AND CONVENTIONS, you hear the finest organizations under the direction of recognized leaders. Don't overlook rehearsals of massed groups and clinic sessions. The guest conductors brought in for these clinics have much to offer, and a record of their remarks, ideas, devices, etc., will prove invaluable.

8 INCLUDE AUDIO-VISUAL AIDS DEALING WITH THE VOICE, choral singing, solo singing, choral groups, and the like in your year's work. They are usually available for a nominal rental fee.

9 IF A DANCE GROUP IS TO PERFORM WITH YOUR CHOIR, tape the selections that are going to be used and send it to the dance group director for use with his group. This will save considerable time as the choral and dance units will not have to rehearse together until *immediately before the program.*

10 INSTRUMENTAL BACKGROUNDS to combined choral and band or orchestra selections can be recorded and made available to the choir director for his use during rehearsal periods. This preliminary use of the instrumental background will condition the choristers to the sound they will eventually hear when all the forces are merged.

11 IF MALE AND FEMALE GROUPS REHEARSE SEPARATELY but desire to combine into a mixed group at a later date, they can record their own parts and then exchange tapes. By use of these taped "other parts" they will orient themselves to the whole *before* the groups combine.

12 USE A TAPE RECORDER FOR TRYOUTS for special groups or solo spots. One forgets the sound of a voice if it is heard at the beginning of a tryout session unless it is exceptionally fine or unusually poor. The voices that are most equal in quality cause the most trouble. A playback of the tryouts with the opportunity to make immediate and convenient comparisons will minimize the problem considerably. The tape itself serves as "evidence" should any question as to your decision be raised.

13 PLAN TO USE A SMALL PORTION OF YOUR ANNUAL BUDGET FOR THE PURCHASE OF RECORDINGS of outstanding choral groups.

Choral directors should be professionally aware of the choral records that are available. In addition to those released by record companies, these are some of the other sources:

a) Albums made by fine college groups. These are usually for sale and often include many excellent choral selections that can readily be performed by high school, community and church groups. If these are not available through your local dealer, contact the college book stores or the music department for further information.

b) Each state has several semi-professional concerns whose business it is to record All-State, District, County Festivals and the like. Many of these recordings, particularly at the All-State level, are well done and can be purchased reasonably.

c) Many good high school choirs, as well as community and church organizations, record their groups from year to year and sell these recordings to raise money for worthy projects.

d) Some community Public Libraries have instituted a record lending service. Ask the librarian to purchase some choral recordings and make these recordings "assigned listening" for the members of your chorus.

CHAPTER **16**

PROGRAM AND PERFORMANCE SUGGESTIONS

USE OF INSTRUMENTS

1 USE CHORAL SELECTIONS WHERE YOUR ACCOMPANIST HAS THE OPPORTUNITY TO BE CO-FEATURED. (Malaguena — Lecuona, *E. B. Marks.*)

2 USE WORKS THAT CALL FOR SOLO OR ENSEMBLE, INSTRUMENTAL BACKGROUND OTHER THAN, OR IN ADDITION TO PIANO.

a) Additional obbligato instruments (Violin Duet) (The Snow—Elgar, *Choral Art Co.*)

b) Instrumental accompaniment other than piano (Harp). (Ceremony of Carols, *Boosey & Hawkes, Inc.*).

c) Small rhythm groups (drums bass, guitar) are effective with standard or popular tunes (I Got Rhythm — Gershwin, *Music Publishers Holding Corp.*)

d) Rhythm and color instruments (guitar, bongo drums, maracas, etc.) add charm to Latin American music (Tico Tico — Simeone, *Shawnee Press*) or American and other folk songs (Cindy — arr. Wilson, *Hall, McCreary Co.*).

e) Brass ensembles can be added to many straight-forward chorale tunes (Break Forth O Beauteous Heavenly Light — Bach, *Bourne Music Co.*).

f) String quartet is effective with quiet, more restrained choral numbers (Ave Verum — Mozart, *any edition;* Elegy — Beethoven, *E. B. Marks*).

g) Many religious selections sound different when accompanied by organ rather than piano. If the school does not own an organ it is often possible to rent an electric organ for a modest fee.

3 COMBINE THE CHORUS WITH BAND OR ORCHESTRA. If the instrumental groups are not competent or, do not exist, explore the instrumental possibilities among the adults of the community.

If instrumental accompaniments are not available in printed form, request permission from the publisher to make your *own* arrangement. In most cases, permission will be granted. *It is an infringement of copyright to make such an arrangement without permission of the copyright owner.*

4 PROGRAM AN INSTRUMENTAL SOLO OR ENSEMBLE TO VARY A CHORAL PROGRAM. Feature professional, college, or local soloists or groups as well as students. Extra attractions are good publicity and result in a definite musical "lift" for the members of the choir.

CHORAL THEMES

1 USE A "THEME" FOR YOUR CONCERT, a central idea or subject around which your music is selected.

Ex.:

1. "Religious Music of Three Faiths".
2. "Music in Work, Worship and War".
3. "Musical Americana".
4. "South of the Border".

2 HAVE A SHORT "CHORAL THEME" OR "SINGER'S GREETING" FOR YOUR GROUP. (Salutation — Gaines, *J. Fischer Bros.*). Many groups have had choral themes composed for them, in some cases by students. These choral themes usually start the program, sometimes behind a closed curtain, sometimes on a·hum with a narrator welcoming the audience and setting the mood for the program.

The "choral theme" is an excellent warm-up number and helps allay "first number" jitters.

GENERAL CONSIDERATIONS

1 KEEP YOUR PROGRAM SHORT. One hour and fifteen minutes, including intermission, is adequate. If the organizations are superior or if the program has been artistically and cleverly staged, an additional fifteen minutes could be added. Always leave the audience wanting more!

2 USE YOUR BALCONY FOR STRIKING EFFECTS. Antiphonal choirs, descant and instrumental groups can be placed in the balcony and used occasionally to add interest. The younger groups can be incorporated into the program in the same way. minimizing staging difficulties. Use the pit in the same fashion.

3 HAVE A "NAME" SOLOIST FOR YOUR PROGRAMS. Many established "stars" as well as younger artists can be engaged for a reasonable fee. The cost of bringing a "name" to your community can be reduced by your arranging an itinerary for the artist with directors in neighboring communities, thus providing several concert appearances in a localized area.

4 REFRAIN FROM REPEATING CHORAL SELECTIONS FROM YEAR TO YEAR. The only exceptions should be the "choral theme", the "traditional" repeater, or numbers that are strongly requested. Directors have a very short period of contact with their choir members and owe it to them to give them as much *different* fine music as is possible in that brief time. Why not set up a three or four year course of study which would include representative compositions of all periods and styles of choral writing.

5 START YOUR PROGRAMS ON TIME.

6 MAKE CERTAIN THAT YOUR CHOIR MEMBERS ATTEND CONCERTS BY OUTSTANDING ARTISTS if they appear in your vicinity.

7 TRY AN INFORMAL CONCERT. Invite parents and guests to an open rehearsal.

8 INVITE OTHER LOCAL CONDUCTORS to rehearse and conduct your groups.

9 INVITE OTHER SCHOOL OR CHURCH GROUPS to share your public presentation.

10 DO NOT CONDUCT YOUR ACCOMPANIST DURING INTERLUDES, POSTLUDES, AND THE LIKE.

11 TRAIN YOUR CHOIR TO TAKE PITCHES PROFESSIONALLY WHEN PERFORMING UNAC- COMPANIED SELECTIONS. The procedure is to have a pitch pipe placed in the hands of a dependable member of the group. During the applause, he blows the pitch of the root of the chord of the next piece to be performed. From this note, the choir members take their starting notes. If the *first* number of a pro- gram is unaccompanied, the starting notes are usually given *offstage*.

If the group cannot sing a chord from a root tone, place a pitch pipe in *each* section to give the individual notes of the chord. Make certain the pitch pipes are in tune with each other on *all* notes.

The procedure of taking new pitches relatively from the ending of the previous selection is a difficult one to master and should perhaps be reserved for profes- sional and college groups.

12 SING A SELECTION THROUGH AT LEAST TWICE WITHOUT ERROR BEFORE IT IS PER- FORMED IN PUBLIC.

13 HAVE YOUR ENSEMBLES AND SOLOISTS PERFORM THEIR NUMBERS PUBLICLY BEFORE SINGING THEM AT CONTESTS AND FESTIVALS.

a) Let them perform before the choir itself. The director should arrange his rehearsal so that one soloist or ensemble is heard at the conclusion of each of the many rehearsals before the date of the contest. This de- creases the soloist's "jitters" and also gives the choir members contact with good solo and ensemble literature that normally they would not have had. It also stimulates interest in younger choir members to take part in such future events.

b) Present soloists and ensembles in afternoon "recitals." The president of the choir should introduce the soloists, who in turn should announce their own selections and make a few remarks pertinent to them. In- formality is the key word.

c) Schedule an assembly program for the entire student body.

d) Allow students to act as adjudicators for each other. Use official state or national adjudication sheets to establish and define the criteria of evalua- tion. Adjudication sheets are available from central offices at a nominal cost and the expense involved is even less if they are mimeographed.

These adjudication sheets make the student cognizant of the technical and musical aspects of performance, and focus attention not only on the weaknesses in the performance he is evaluating, but on his own weak- nesses (and strengths) as well. This awareness of the many areas of criticism on which they will be graded results in a more intelligent series of practice sessions and a superior performance at festival time.

ABOUT THE NUMBERS

1 USE NARRATION OR CHORIC SPEAKING to supply continuity, either for a complete program or for an occasional number. Some works contain dialogue. By using this type of selection we are able to bring together other school departments or community groups.

2 DO NOT SING TAXING NUMBERS AT THE BEGINNING OF A PROGRAM.

3 DO NOT PLACE COMICAL OR HUMOROUS WORKS IN A GROUP WITH SERIOUS MUSIC. Transitions of mood must be made gracefully.

4 A PROGRAM SHOULD HAVE UNITY AND VARIETY. Numbers in groups should bear a definite unified relationship to each other. Pieces of the same period or type should be grouped together. Variety may·be secured within each group by programming works with contrasting features and styles.

5 DON'T OVERLOOK A SOFT NUMBER AS A CONCLUDING WORK. It is natural to save your "big" numbers for the end of a group or large section, but oftimes moods are created by ending a program on a quiet note.

6 PREPARE AN ENCORE, but don't use it unless there is a definite demand for it.

7 INCLUDE SEVERAL A CAPPELLA SELECTIONS ON EVERY PROGRAM. While there is a tendency to draw from the polyphonic schools for these works, one should not forget that there are many fine contemporary works written for a cappella rendition.

8 DO NOT USE THE ENTIRE CHORUS WHEN PRESENTING MADRIGALS, GLEES, AND SIMILAR COMPOSITIONS. While some of these works do "come off" with a large group, they are essentially chamber music types and demand presentation by small ensembles.

Incidentally, do not present more than *one* group of this type of composition on any one concert program.

9 IF YOU MUST PREPARE A PROGRAM IN A SHORT PERIOD OF TIME, TRY THE FOLLOWING:

    1. Use numbers that contain many unison passages.

    2. Use numbers that have incidental solo spots.

    3. Use numbers where male voices have the melody and female voices the harmony.

    4. MANY EXTENDED FOUR PART NUMBERS (Medleys, fantasies, etc.,) LEND THEMSELVES TO SIMPLIFICATION by the following devices:

        a) Sing certain sections in *unison* rather than in *parts* as arranged. Good color can be secured by having a phrase or section sung by the female voices, following by a section sung by the male voices, followed by the two in unison. If desired, the actual part harmony as written in the score can be used for a "splash" ending on the last four measures of the section. This is a common radio and television procedure, when much material must be quickly absorbed by the performers.

        b) Assign a section to a *soloist* or *rescore* a four part harmony section into a *two part duet* between a male and female voice. There is always a spot for this type of change in many of the fine show tune medleys now available in print.

c) Have a *quartet* or small *ensemble* sing one section rather than the full chorus. An ensemble can usually learn its assigned section with little assistance from the director and the additional rehearsal time gained will be invaluable.